the art of promotion

CREATING DISTINCTION THROUGH INNOVATIVE PRODUCTION TECHNIQUES

Lisa L. Cyr

GLOUCESTER MASSACHUSETTS

ROCKPORT PUBLISHERS

First published in the United States of America by Rockport Publishers, Inc., a member of Quayside Publishing Group
33 Commercial Street
Gloucester, Massachusetts 01930-5089
Telephone: (978) 282-9590
Fax: (978) 283-2742
www.rockpub.com

Library of Congress Cataloging-in-Publication Data available

ISBN 1-59253-186-5

10 9 8 7 6 5 4 3 2 1

Design: Art & Anthropology
Cover Image: Art & Anthropology

Printed in China

p n

ROCKPORT

I would like to give special thanks to all the creatives who contributed to this book. Their profound courage in venturing out with a unique voice and vision make this book an inspiration to all. Kudos to my editor, Kristin Ellison, for her keen eye, wonderful sense of humor, and love of books, which always make a project such as this a pleasure to do. I would also like to thank my family for instilling in me the love of creativity, self-expression, and the importance of sharing my gifts with others.

All things can be done for the one who believes.
Mark 9:23

the art of promotion

CREATING DISTINCTION THROUGH INNOVATIVE PRODUCTION TECHNIQUES

Introduction

positioning yourself in the creative marketplace

With the overall decline in the global economy, many creatives find themselves at a crossroad. Work is no longer abundant, and budgets have decreased significantly from years past. In the boom of the early 1990s, the biggest concern for most was simply coping with the workload and managing growth. In today's volatile marketplace, creatives now face many more challenges. To survive, they are reevaluating their approach to promotion and restructuring their position in the marketplace. They are beginning to take an honest look not only at how they work, what they have to uniquely offer, and the markets and clients they choose to work with but also introspectively at their creative interests and aspirations, belief system, and their definition of what it means to be successful. In these uncertain times, many are pausing to reshape their business so as to enrich their lives.

To combat the instability in the marketplace, many creatives are choosing to venture into entrepreneurial initiatives. They are transcending traditional nomenclature to discover new markets and diversify their offerings. Everything from direct-to-consumer merchandising, self-publishing, and licensing are being explored. To stay on top of future opportunities, many are adopting an ongoing research component as a part of their regular planning process.

When it comes to promotion, creating distinction is key. Because of the tremendous distractions going on in the world, promotions need to be truly unique and thought-provoking in order to capture the attention of any audience. To create distinction and call attention to their brand, creatives are producing memorable promotions that reveal something about their firm and its personality. These are not only highly innovative from a production standpoint but also keenly strategic where the overall messaging is mindful of a prospective client's needs. Many promotions serve secondary functions—as demonstrations of a firm's capabilities or as keepsakes that significantly increase longevity and effectiveness. Creatives are rethinking function and making strides into what is possible in form.

Many are realizing the importance of contact strategies in an age where electronic communication has become prevalent. To make their promotions more personalized, many firms are no longer producing mass mailings but instead creating smaller, more targeted promotions. They are also thinking in terms of a campaign, uniting all their messaging and correspondence to ensure clarity and consistency within the marketplace. Follow-up procedures are also becoming a regular part of the process. To maintain that vital connection with prospective and existing clients, creatives are finding almost any notable occasion worthy of a promotional message, from moving announcements, anniversary celebrations, and holiday greetings to the announcement of awards and achievements and the addition of new staff members. Personalized thank-you notes and expressions of gratitude are also going a long way in making lasting impressions with clients. Many firms are hiring personnel to cultivate new business, and more time is being given to other forms of promotion, like networking and public relations. After the events of September 11, 2001, people in general are seeing the need to work together—and creatives are also beginning to appreciate the benefits of collaboration. They are starting to focus their efforts on internal team-building as well as establishing relationships with sources outside their discipline.

Whether a company is new and embarking on a launch or a seasoned firm in the midst of a rebranding effort, market positioning can be challenging. It requires intensive thought and focus, evaluation, planning, and commitment in order to move forward. But for those who are willing to venture out with a unique voice and vision, it can be an enlightening and even empowering experience. Don't allow yourself to get caught up in the day-to-day so much that you lose sight of what is important. You have the power within you to design your own creative path and business future. Just remember to focus, plan, commit—and, most of all, believe in yourself.

unconventional and printing

surfaces
ing techniques

There is an ever-growing interest in exploring unconventional materials, surfaces, and techniques to create distinction. Creatives are looking to sources outside the communications industry, and they are finding interesting alternatives. They are experimenting with various techniques on a vast array of materials from metal, wood, and plastic to leather, handmade and custom paper, and laminated duplexes of every kind. Tactile processes like etching, laser cutting, sculpted embossing, and embroidery are becoming more widely used, and old techniques like wood type and letterpress are being revisited. Inks are glowing in the dark, glitter infused, heat sensitive, and scratching off to reveal an underlying message. Print is also becoming more animated with lenticular printing and three-dimensional with anaglyphic stereo usage. Technological innovations make the possibilities endless.

To keep abreast of what is out there, build relationships with suppliers from different disciplines and collect catalogs from myriad sources. Most importantly, don't be afraid to make mistakes when you are treading new ground. "The fear of making mistakes will always bring you to walk in the middle of the road," comments designer Mirko Ilić. "I always give myself the freedom to make mistakes in order for something unusual to happen." Finding new ways to combine different materials and techniques can give any project the edge that it needs to stand out in the marketplace.

marking
freedom

The construction that houses the calendar is heavy and blocklike to symbolize a wall. Throughout the solid structure is hand-lettering, a unique mixture of Latin and Cyrillic characters, giving the text an Eastern European flair. Specially mixed ink is used to imprint the letters, simulating the look of graphite. Glow-in-the-dark ink is also applied, illuminating the bricks of a wall. On the spine, two die-cut holes imply something interesting inside. The piece is written in both the English and Serbian language.

Every year since 1993, Publikum, a major printing company in Belgrade, produces a calendar of exceptional artistic merit that traditionally featured Yugoslavia's artistic heritage and rich pop culture. However, by 2001 many things had changed, and the calendar needed to reflect the new era. For Serbians, it was a new world without boundaries. "I started to work on the calendar in the year they brought down Milosevic," says designer Mirko Ilić. "I was in charge of developing the concept, and my first idea was to bring in something new, fresh ideas and new people, for an exchange of things to happen." With the concept of overcoming barriers at the forefront, Ilić entitled the calendar *ANTIWALL*. With the goal of opening doors to different perspectives, the imagery was selected to really push the envelope, be innovative, and, most importantly, take risks. Artists from all over the world were asked to submit work. Twelve were chosen, one for each month.

To communicate the weight and solidity of a wall, Ilić designed a construction that was almost blocklike to house the calendar of new life and contemporary art. "I wanted it to look like a part of the wall, like one of the bricks," he comments. Glow-in-the-dark ink was used throughout the piece to represent a beacon of light for those still trying to find a way out of the darkness. "One is a physical wall and the other is a wall that you create for yourself," explains Ilić. To protect the ink from being scratched, the front and back covers of the book were laminated. Two holes were die-cut from the spine as a device to entice the viewer to explore further.

From the left-hand side pocket, the square-shaped calendar unfolds. The stunning cover reveals a glow-in-the-dark wall with the names of the participating artists peering through. The images, thought-provoking and controversial, help illuminate each month, reveling in the vast opportunities that a new day brings. All the text is hand-lettered to give the project a human touch. To achieve this, Ilić designed a custom font, set the type in Quark, outputted at 150 percent, and had his staff laboriously trace each page in pencil onto translucent paper. Each sheet of tracing paper was then scanned into the computer and reduced to the appropriate size, giving the project a unique, handcrafted look.

Conceived with the idea that art has the power to promote change, the bilingual 2001 calendar serves not only as a reminder of the turmoil and destruction of the past but also as a source for inspiration and hope in the potential that a world without boundaries brings. At a televised celebration, the calendars were stacked like bricks in a wall. They were given to a select group of people, as were specifically designed shopping bags that also glowed in the dark. Exactly 2,001 calendars were produced.

TECHNICAL TIPS

Glow-in-the-dark ink is made by mixing translucent ink with a special powder. The surface can glow for long periods in the dark and has a shelf life of about two to five years, depending on where the printed piece is kept. To obtain the most luminosity from the specialty ink, make sure it is applied directly on a white surface. Use an overall varnish or lamination to seal and protect the surface.

When you are creating a unique construction, make several prototypes, analyzing the piece from the perspective of the recipient. If you want to avoid fold marks, try a heavy perforation that stops shy of the sides of the paper; this allows the calendar to fold away nicely without leaving a mark once it's hung on a wall. It also adds a nice decorative accent to the page.

DO IT FOR LESS

Many of the unique features of this piece were executed by hand. Using a standard font instead of hand-lettering would save tremendously in labor costs. To cut costs further, the calendar itself could be made smaller, eliminating the need for perforation.

When you open the piece, you see markings—2001, to be exact—that symbolize many years in captivity. The text, which begins in English and ends in Serbian, reads "The time is now." A perfect-bound book of new art and contemporary life is adhered to the right side. Inside the left-hand pocket lies a matching glow-in-the-dark calendar. To ensure that unwanted folds would not remain once the calendar is fully open, the designer utilizes a heavy perforation instead of a score. Loose cardboard is positioned in the back to keep the calendar erect; a wire rod is placed inside the spiral binding, allowing the piece to hang.

2

1

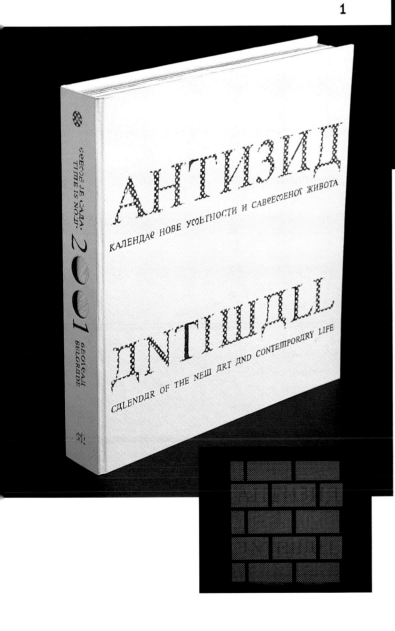

FIRM: MIRKO ILIĆ CORPORATION

CREATIVE DIRECTOR: STANISLAV SHARP, FIA ART GROUP

PROJECT COORDINATOR: NADA RAJIČIĆ FIA ART GROUP

DESIGNER/FONT DESIGNER: MIRKO ILIĆ

HAND LETTERING: MIRKO ILIĆ, RINGO TAKAHASHI, RYUTA NAKAZAWA, ASA HASIMOTO, AND JELENA ČAMBA DJORDJEVIĆ

ILLUSTRATION: SLAVIMIR STOJANOVIĆ

FEATURED ARTISTS: WIM WENDERS, VIK MUNIZ, BJORK, DRAGON ZIVADINOV, NATACHA MERRITT, MARINA ABRAMOVIĆ, BARBARA KRUGER, AES GROUP, TADANORI YOKOO, OLIVIERO TOSCANI, CHRISTO AND JEANNE-CLAUDE, AND DAVID BYRNE

PRINTING AND BINDERY: PUBLIKUM

wood type: redefined

A simple, yet elegant, brochure is used to promote a limited-edition series of typographic prints by designer Dennis Y. Ichiyama. Each brochure is housed in a three-panel, letterpress-printed wrap that piques curiosity, enticing the reader to investigate further. Inside, background information on the artist's experience at the museum and the work he created unfolds. Each four-color image was made with a Xerox technology.

After an artist-in-residence stay at the Hamilton Wood Type & Printing Museum, designer and educator Dennis Y. Ichiyama was hooked. Since 1999, he has been working with wood type, redefining its traditional nomenclature and reintroducing the almost extinct process back into the culture. "Its history and tradition are imbedded in stereotypical references that make for a great challenge," says Ichiyama.

With over a million pieces of wood type and ornaments to choose from, Ichiyama rolled up his sleeves and went to work. Free to determine his own design problem and approach, he seized the opportunity to play and experiment. "Rather than to letter a word, text, or paragraph, I decided that the letterforms themselves were interesting and unique enough just as shapes," he recalls. "They took me back to a period of my childhood when letters were combinations of curves, angles, horizontals, and verticals that did not create words but compositions of form and color."

Pure Type Forms, a series of typographic limited-edition prints, was the result of Ichiyama's efforts. Each print explores the elegance and beauty that wood type can bring to a surface. As a finishing touch, they are signed, dated, and imprinted in red with the artist's family seal. "I have always felt that as a designer I want to blend East and West," adds Ichiyama. "Whenever I sign my work, I sign it in both a Western calligraphic form and a geometric eastern form with my seal." The series of prints is housed in a custom presentation folder, adding elegance to the overall package.

To promote the work, a simple, yet elegant, brochure was created and presented within a three-panel, letterpress-printed wrap. Inside the accordion-folded brochure, the artist and his experience with wood type was revealed. To be cost effective, the four-color images within the brochure were photocopied and hand-tipped into each piece.

Ichiyama's most recent work, entitled *More Pure Type Forms*, evolved from typographic experimentation to the design of limited-edition keepsakes. To present these latest endeavors to the marketplace, the designer developed another promotional package. To maintain continuity, the overall design and format are consistent with the first promotion.

Because of Ichiyama's efforts, printing with wood type, once a vintage process, has now been rejuvenated and brought back to the masses for many to enjoy for years to come. "For me, it has been a low-tech activity that stirs the emotions and the soul," shares Ichiyama. "My course in typography [at Purdue University] has been enriched and my approach to graphic design has been expanded."

TECHNICAL TIPS

When working with wood type, do not expect perfection. Instead, embrace the wonderful irregularities and transparent overlays it creates. After several rounds of wiping and reinking, an interesting patina develops on the wood surface that gives an artistic quality to the resulting impression. If you are interested in knowing more about the history of wood type or obtaining access to a diverse collection, the Hamilton Wood Type & Printing Museum is a wonderful place to start.

The portfolio contains typographic artwork printed on superfine, soft white 80-lb. and ultrawhite, smooth 65-lb. cover using the museum's Vandercook SP 15 letterpress. Each print is housed inside a folder labeled with the appropriate number in silver. An introduction is also included to help explain the experimental endeavor. Everything is packaged in a three-panel, letter-folded wrap.

To present his most recent work, the designer developed a second promotional package. This brochure focuses on the development of limited-edition keepsakes created in conjunction with several events. Presented here are prints for the Society of Typographic Arts, the University of Reading's conference on printing history, and a remembrance piece from the tragedy of September 11, 2001 entitled *Tribute in Light*. For the sake of continuity, the design and format are consistent with that of the first promotion.

Because of the attention the typographic work has generated, the artist has been asked to work on several outside projects. This keepsake was created to celebrate the seventy-fifth anniversary of the Society of Typographic Arts.

1

FIRM: DENNIS Y. ICHIYAMA

CREATIVE DIRECTOR AND DESIGNER:
DENNIS Y. ICHIYAMA

ILLUSTRATION: DENNIS Y. ICHIYAMA

PRINTING: HAMILTON WOOD TYPE &
PRINTING MUSEUM

2

3

4

plainly stated

The promotional ensemble is contained in a silk-screened, standard-size box. When you open the box, you are presented with an introduction card that is individually numbered with a letterpress printing process. The piece closes with a reply card that can be sent back to the design firm for follow-up purposes. An overview brochure provides insight to the history of the New England—based firm and the origins of the name Plainspoke. The piece is shipped in a corrugated material that wraps around and seals at the ends. Only one thousand pieces were produced.

"Plainspoke is a little different. As a name, it stands out, and we wanted to build upon that," shares art director and designer Matt Ralph. "With this promotion, I wanted to do something that was clever, well designed, and that would really make an impact. I did not want it to be hard sell, with a laundry list of capabilities. I wanted our greatness to come through in the quality of the piece." Because the firm was also looking to expand into new markets, the promotion had to be flexible enough for projects to be added or changed as necessary. Using various papers, bindery, and formats, the design firm developed an interesting promotional ensemble based on their distinctive name. "We thought it would be fun to create a kit of things where everything was built upon the whole idea of *plain*," Ralph adds.

To get the concept off the ground, the design team began with a brainstorming session, thinking of objects that could be associated with the word *plain*. Using the plain box as a point of departure, they chose an array of pieces that were interesting, different in shape and texture, and that fit inside a standard-size box. The resulting collection—a Plainspoke company brochure, a plain sight eye chart, a plain bag of notecards and envelopes, plain pencils, a plain pages notebook, and plain flashcards—all fit nicely inside a plain box. Each piece within the promotional package utilizes a different material and printing surface. The silk-screened bag provides a rugged texture while the flashcards bring a glossy finish to the overall matte presentation. The bindery ranges from the traditional saddle-stitching of the company brochure and the spiral-bound notebook to the less typical ring-bound flashcards and the drawstring bag. When you open the promotion, you are immediately presented with an introduction card that describes the contents as "a celebration of all things plain." The piece closes with a reply card that is user-friendly and quite entertaining, as it plays up on the *plain* concept one last time. "The piece is one big hit, and it really makes an impression," admits Ralph.

With this idea-driven collection, Plainspoke was not only able to make their name memorable through repetition of message but also to showcase to clients an array of reproductive possibilities. Because the piece was designed to be flexible, the *plain* concept can be extended to smaller promotions that can be sent more frequently. "With some clients, you just need to work on them overtime," Ralph points out.

TECHNICAL TIPS

To ensure your package comes together in the end, start with your outside container and build the promotion to fit within it. Keep your ideas to a simple theme and vary the textures and shapes for visual interest.

DO IT FOR LESS

If you are doing a small run, digital printing is the way to go. You can also save money by keeping the paper selections to a minimum and assembling each piece in-house.

3

The plain sight eye chart positions Plain-spoke, as the solution to a prospective client's creative needs. The accordion-folded chart conveniently pulls out from a custom-designed sleeve. The grommet allows the piece to be hung if desired.

The silk-screened plain bag contains note-cards, envelopes, and vellum sheets. The pencils are housed in a glassine envelope and sealed with a label. The plain pages note-book is spiral-bound; a wraparound label adorns the cover.

The retro-looking flashcards, printed on 18-point Chromolux 700 paper that is coated on one side, provides a fun and upbeat accent to the presentation. Printed in an array of soft tones, the flashcards continue the plain theme, cleverly utilizing word and image to deliver the message. Each card is drilled and bound with a ring.

1

FIRM: PLAINSPOKE

ART DIRECTOR: MATT RALPH

DESIGNERS: MATT RALPH AND NICOLE COMTOIS

PHOTOGRAPHY: BRIAN WILDER AND VARIOUS STOCK

PRINTING: PENMOR LITHOGRAPHERS (COMPANY BROCHURE, FLASHCARDS, LABEL, NOTECARDS, AND ENVELOPES), MARAN PRINTING SERVICE (EYE CHART, INTRODUCTION CARD, AND REPLY CARD), BLUE DOLPHIN SCREENPRINT (CLOTH BAG)

MANUFACTURERS: MASON BOX COMPANY (KRAFT BOX), SHIP-IT (CLOTH BAG), AMERICAN PRINTING AND ENVELOPE COMPANY (GLASSINE ENVELOPE), ROBBINS CONTAINER CORP. (CORRUGATED MAILING WRAP), AND CYRK (BLACK PENCILS)

4

2

organized
for success

"Most of the time, our clients are looking for us to take charge of a project, so we looked for ways to facilitate that," admits creative director Dann Ilicic. To get their clients and their staff focused and organized for success, the branding firm decided that a notebook would be the perfect vehicle. "We want to communicate that the whole process of branding is really about getting things organized so everybody can understand what needs to be done," Ilicic explains. "The whole notion of the notebook is to get both sides to know what questions to ask."

With the desired format underway, the next challenge was deciding on just the right look and feel. As part of their identity, the company had already produced business cards made of stainless steel. These were such a hit with existing and prospective clientele that it seemed appropriate to produce the notebook in the same material. However, when they tried to use the metal surface as a notebook cover, they realized it was much too heavy a substrate and was crushing the binding coils. After further research, the design team identified a better alternative: lightweight aluminum. The new material had the desired metallic look and feel, but without excess weight—a perfect solution. The 7 $\frac{1}{2}$- by 9 $\frac{1}{2}$-inch (19 by 24 centimeter) metal notebook was laser-cut with the company's logo and polished with sandpaper for a brushed look. Rounded corners were carried throughout to avoid sharp edges and keep the notebook smooth to the touch. An indention on the cover allowed easy access to the inside pages. To save money, the back cover was made of a heavy black stock.

Inside the notebook lies the heart of the project. When it comes to making things happen, Wow! believes you have to be clear about your desired outcome, know your next action, and assign responsibility and deadlines to each task. "It has been our experience that if people can't answer those questions, chances are the desired outcome will not be achieved," claims Ilicic. With this principle in mind, the design team developed an easy-to-use process whereby the user merely plugs in responses to certain simplified questions. Each spread was not only visually interesting but also highly functional. "Our company is called Wow! and one of the things we promote is creating distinction," shares Ilicic. "The desired response is to have clients look at us and think, 'Wow! These people are really thinking.'" Always given out personally at client meetings and presentations, the notebook serves as an excellent vehicle for making any desired outcome a reality.

TECHNICAL TIPS

Laser-cutting is a good way to carve into a metal surface. To smooth out any rough edges, sandpapering or tumbling can be done. You can choose from a variety of metallic surfaces; experiment, trying different weights and finishes, to get the exact look you want.

1

The metal notebook cover is laser-cut and polished for a brushed effect. The book is wire-o bound with two pieces, giving the cover added support to prevent it from warping. The notebook is given to new and existing clients and is also used internally by the staff.

2

The action-driven notebook helps the branding firm and its clients get mobilized by asking a series of questions. To maintain the highest level of detail, the inside is stochastic printed. The firm created a two-color effect on an essentially one-color job by using a stock with a preprinted grid pattern—70-lb. Strathmore Elements text.

1

2

FIRM: WOW! A BRANDING COMPANY

CREATIVE DIRECTOR: DANN ILICIC

DESIGNER: PERRY CHUA

PRINTING: GENERATION PRINTING LTD. (NOTEBOOK TEXT PAGES)

BINDERY: WARD DIGITAL

SPECIAL TECHNIQUES AND MANUFACTURER:

INDUSTRIAL LASER CUTTING (METAL)

play on words

A clear foil stamp accents the 20-point matte Calendered vinyl cover. The pressure and heat used in the stamping process also created a nice debossed effect, an unexpected bonus.

Creative director and illustrator Bob Hambly wanted to create a highly imaginative self-promotion to show off his graphic signature style. "It all started with my sketchbook," he recalls. "I was fooling around with words and I came up with the idea of creating arranged marriages." Out of a list of about fifty potential ideas, the artist selected those with the most broadest-based appeal. Working on a light table with a big chiseled marker, Hambly brought to life his creative play on words. Once he was satisfied with the gesture and look of the line art, each image was then scanned into the computer, streamlined, and colored. Using a diverse range of subject matter, Hambly developed fifteen hybrid images that cleverly illustrate how two seemingly opposing objects can be put together. "It helps to have a theme or a storyline to show art directors that you can solve a problem as opposed to just showing pretty pictures," he adds.

With an interesting collection of words and images under his belt, Hambly's next challenge was to put them together in a package that enhanced the illustrative content. "Because I work in a design studio, I am surrounded by lots of materials and promotions. One in particular, a paper promotion, used plastic that was not only silk-screen-printed but also embossed and debossed. It intrigued me, and I told my printer about it," notes Hambly. Working collaboratively, the printer and illustrator experimented with several effects. The result features a clear foil stamp that gives dimension to the illustrated plastic cover.

To maintain the cover's velvety look and feel, the interior illustrated pages are laminated. "Knowing that the pages would be constantly turning and pivoting, we wanted to make sure we put a coating over the ink so it would not scratch," offers Hambly. The interior was printed on Utopia One dull cover using a metallic blue and dark brown palette. The overall piece was trimmed with a custom die and bound with Chicago screws. To ensure that each page lined up perfectly, the hole that helps bind the piece was punched out as part of the die; drilling would have left too much room for error in the final product. The circular die around the binding, the rounded corners, and the circular page numbers work together to highlight the illustrator's fluid line work and soften the overall graphic presentation. "People will always want to keep and remember something that is well done," concludes Hambly. "The idea, execution, materials, and all the little details and final touches are important because they speak indirectly about how much you care about your work."

TECHNICAL TIPS

When blind-embossing plastic, it is important to run tests on the material. If the pressure is too strong, the plastic will crack, ripple, and warp. If it is not strong enough, you will not be able to see what you are applying to the surface. Die-cutting windows or shapes into the interior of plastic is not a forgiving technique, as the cut marks can be quite evident.

DO IT FOR LESS

By eliminating the plastic cover, you could save quite a bit. Instead of laminating each page, a varnish could be applied to both sides. Getting rid of the rounded edges and the need for a custom die would also save money.

The illustrated promotion is printed on Utopia One dull cover in metallic blue and dark brown. To ensure solid coverage, the brown is double hit. Each page is coated with matte OPP laminate (1.5 millimeter) as a visual and tactile tie to the plastic cover. The coating also helps protect the pages from scratches and tears.

The simple graphic renderings challenge the viewer's perception in a smart, attractive fashion. On the back, the associated word-play is revealed.

1

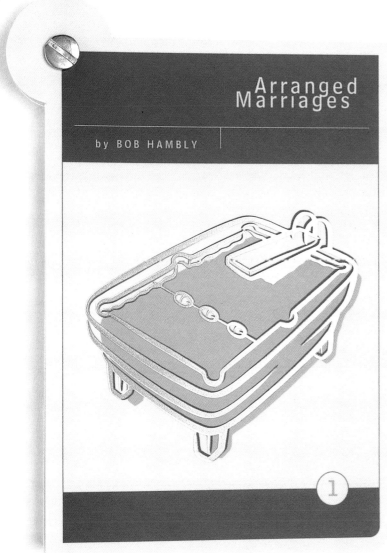

2

3

FIRM: HAMBLY & WOOLLEY, INC.

CREATIVE DIRECTOR: BOB HAMBLY

DESIGNERS: JASON ZALESKI AND ROB WILSON

ILLUSTRATION: BOB HAMBLY

PRINTING: SOMERSET GRAPHICS CO. LTD.

putting
creativity
to work

Over the last decade, Jason & Jason Visual Communications has experienced substantial and continuous growth not only in the staff they employ but also in the clients they serve. To more accurately reflect their global expansion and full-service capabilities, the communications firm set their sights on an extensive marketing campaign, including a highly impressive promotional kit to be used by the sales staff. "It is just one part of a highly focused and comprehensive sales and marketing program we embarked on three years ago when we launched our Web site," notes creative director Jonathan Jason. "Since that time, we have been engaged in direct marketing: e-mail campaigns, direct mail, promotional give-aways, print advertising, and personal telemarketing."

After researching and analyzing their internal operations, existing client base, and the overall competitive landscape, the firm concluded that "we needed to communicate who we are and what we do, showing tangibles and backing up our claims with client case studies and projects," shares Jason. "This meant being able to present our value proposition in a way that would allow our customers to see and understand for themselves the added value of working with a company like ours." The firm also needed to reposition themselves from a "passive supplier of commodity-like promotional items to an active provider of creative and customer-focused business solutions," Jason adds. "Great Ideas at Work" became the title and slogan of the project. When applied to secondary messaging like "Focus Your Vision, Build Your Brand, and Empower Your Company," the promotion really pinpointed the value that Jason & Jason Visual Communications could bring to any company.

With clearly defined objectives and a solid marketing strategy in place, the firm focused on the promotion's hierarchy and dissemination of information. To keep the content simple and organized, it was divided into three independently functioning pieces—a company overview brochure, a projects and supportive case studies brochure, and a new works booklet—that could also work together as a cohesive unit. "Breaking the material into sections helps the reader compartmentalize relevant information that may otherwise be lost," offers Jason. "In addition, we felt a project presentation made of multiple pieces was more interesting and gave the reader a feeling of being on a journey." The multipieced assemblage not only makes the presentation interactive but also gives maximum flexibility when material requires updating and revision, increasing the longevity of the promotion. In addition, an enclosed CD-ROM provides access to the company's multimedia presentation, a way to disseminate current information to interested parties.

TECHNICAL TIPS

To achieve subtle variations of silver, overprint fields of color beneath the metallic ink. In this promotional package, black is printed under the silver to achieve the darker tintlike effect. The look is much softer than that of overprinting tints of black on the silver, which also dulls and decreases the metallic look of the ink. Working creatively with metallic inks requires a lot of experimentation, as no controlled approach yields an accurate reading by using a proof alone. If you intend to work with metallic inks frequently, begin to track test results from actual print runs. This will provide you with an indispensable indication of how the inks behave in a variety of applications. It is also a good idea to consult with your printer, who has a wealth of experience to share.

If you intend to use UV lacquer as a graphic element in your work, you may want to make the treatment more noticeable by backing it with a 3 to 5 percent color tint with direct-to-plate production and a 10 percent tint when using traditional film-produced plates.

When laminating both sides of a project that also must be folded, the piece may tend to spring back slightly. In this case, it may be more effective to laminate one side and lacquer the other. Make sure to produce an accurate mock-up to avoid surprises. Laminating metallic inks covers surface flaws inherent in the paper, giving the piece a more uniform look.

The engaging, three-dimensional presentation folder, entitled *Great Ideas at Work,* houses a company overview brochure with an interactive demo on CD-ROM, a projects brochure, a new works biannual booklet, and a business card. Each piece fits nicely within the package in an almost Mondrian-like fashion. The folder is printed in five colors, process plus PMS 877 silver onto 450-gram Bristol semimatte coated stock. On the cover, the word *inspire* is highlighted through the application of UV lacquer. Inside, chartreuse complements the overall silver color scheme.

Entitled *Define, Develop, Deploy,* the projects brochure presents three case studies and the firm's portfolio of work from a targeted array of industries. Each case study not only includes an overview and strategic objectives but also outlines how the firm solved the communications problem. This is enhanced by a double-page spread highlighting measurable results for the client. The matte-laminated and selective UV-lacquered wraparound cover employs a hidden spiral binding, protecting the pieces within the package from scratches and snags. The piece is organized in three sections separated by French-folded pages.

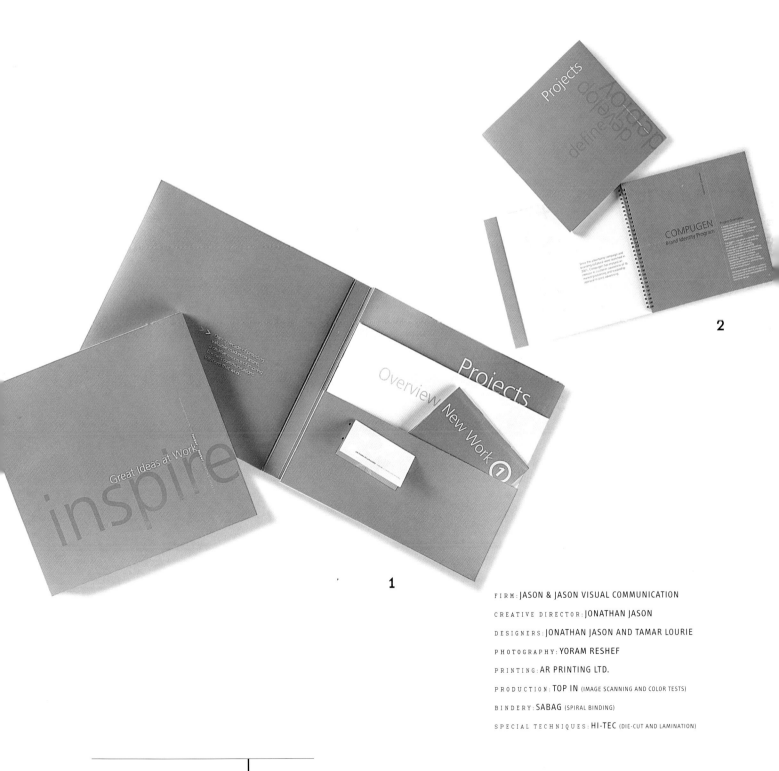

2

1

FIRM: JASON & JASON VISUAL COMMUNICATION

CREATIVE DIRECTOR: JONATHAN JASON

DESIGNERS: JONATHAN JASON AND TAMAR LOURIE

PHOTOGRAPHY: YORAM RESHEF

PRINTING: AR PRINTING LTD.

PRODUCTION: TOP IN (IMAGE SCANNING AND COLOR TESTS)

BINDERY: SABAG (SPIRAL BINDING)

SPECIAL TECHNIQUES: HI-TEC (DIE-CUT AND LAMINATION)

With the content divided into understandable parts, the designers next worked to develop the look and feel of the piece. A square grid design was chosen and the company's existing corporate color scheme and visual brand identity was applied. Throughout the promotional package, design elements repeat from piece to piece, giving the overall presentation a unified look. The messaging, design, and innovation in production were a tribute to the communications firm's keen attention to both strategic and creative detail. The marketing ensemble, a source of pride for the agency, was personally presented to prospective clients—mostly multinational business-to-business companies in the technology, biotechnology, pharmaceuticals, finance, and real estate industries.

DO IT FOR LESS

With a project of this magnitude, look to your suppliers for professional discounts. Increased work for you also results in a surge in work for them—a win-win situation all around. Other ways to reduce costs include maximizing your press sheet, eliminating the film stage of the process by going direct to plate, and utilizing digital photography wherever possible.

3

The corporate overview brochure, designed to function as a stand-alone piece as well, provides prospective clients with insight into the firm's corporate culture, value offerings, international staff, and working methodologies. The booklet employs foldover flaps for both the front and back cover; these not only add structural strength to the piece but also function as bookmarks and convenient places to hold the agency's multimedia presentation CD-ROM and a business card. On the cover, a tinted UV gloss lacquer draws attention to the brochure's theme, entitled *Focus, Build, Empower*. For protection, a matte lamination is applied inside and out.

A minibrochure, entitled *New Work*, is designed to be a cost-effective way to highlight recent work. On the cover, matte lamination is added for durability while a UV lacquer highlights key text and graphic elements on both the front and back. The flaps that extend the cover repeat a design element that echoes through the entire project. This is the first in a series that will be distributed every six months.

4

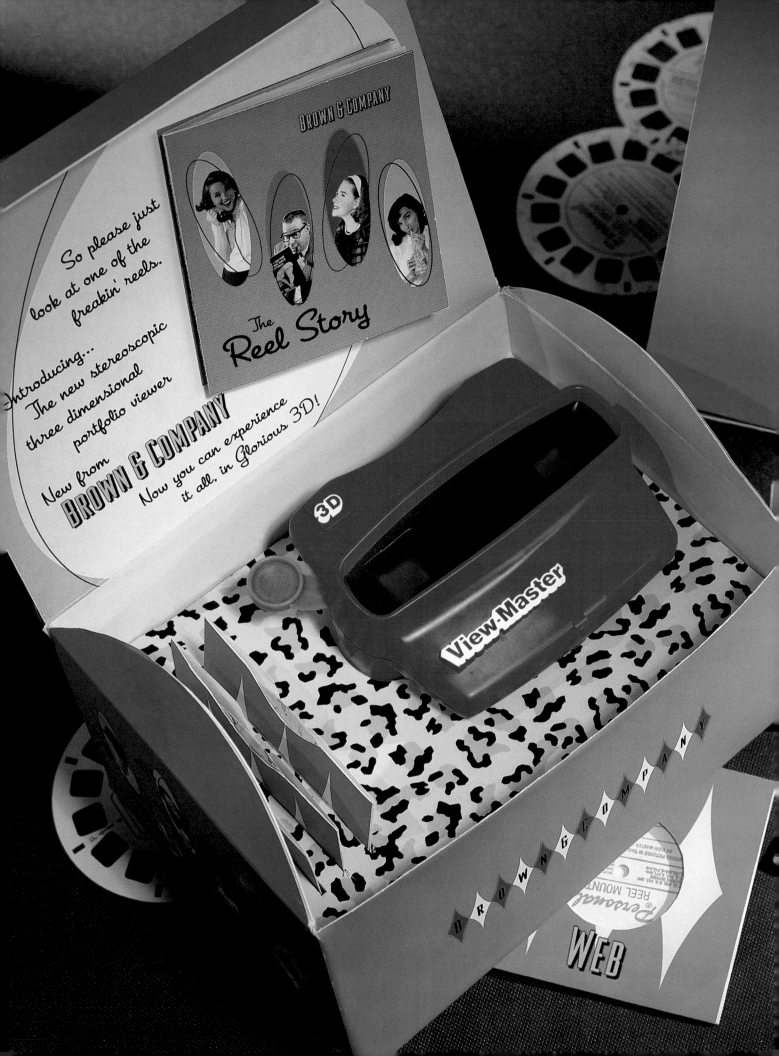

defining your niche

To survive in today's marketplace, you need to establish what makes you different from the competition. The best way to get in tune with your unique voice and vision is to take an honest look at not only your working process and approach, experience and capabilities, and client relations and market preferences but also your core beliefs and values, creative interests, and aspirations. These are, collectively, what make your offerings distinctive. If you present the marketplace with nothing unique, you open yourself up to becoming a sophisticated order taker, leaving the opportunity for buyers to price-shop alternatives. "You have to closely define what your goals are and where you really want to go," says Lars Harmsen of MAGMA. "For us, it was very important to determine our identity before we began working for clients, so that in the first contact, we could communicate our spirit and our meaning of design." By defining your niche, you are setting a foundation on which to strategically position and build your brand.

With an identity clearly delineated, you have a working model to turn to when it comes to promotional messaging. The biggest mistake any firm or freelancer can make is to promote an identity that is not genuine. To project one image and live another will result only in a great lack of authenticity and major disconnections down the road. "The traditional view of branding is that it is the icing on the cake—the logo, colors, and the things that people see. But the branding of the inside—the people, process, and culture—is just as important because it is the repeat business side," observes Dann Ilicic of Wow! A Branding Company. "You must walk the walk as well as talk the talk to make your brand live." For the

creative team at Red Canoe, establishing a clearly defined mission statement was essential to staying focused and on track. Partners Deb Koch and Caroline Kavanagh made the decision early on that it was important to them to break away from the fast-paced, stress-inducing hustle and bustle of the everyday work scene to create an environment that would energize their spirit and fill their soul. A cabin, situated among 350 acres of breathtaking panoramic views, became their tranquil place of business and source of inspiration. Since 1997, Red Canoe's philosophical mission and tagline, "As we live, so we work," has been the foundation that has shaped their business plan to fit and enrich their lives.

Being selective in your approach to new business is key. By developing relationships with clients who share your vision, you begin to build recognition and market value. "In the beginning, we purposely turned away a lot of work, and that was very difficult. But now it has come full circle and we are able to capitalize on being known for what we do," acknowledges Ilicic. "We built a dream list of clients we really wanted to work for, and we purposely pitched those businesses." By actively pursuing work they are sincerely passionate about, the relatively new company has been able to launch their practice into the limelight with numerous accolades. "Doing the work you love begets like-minded clients and projects, creating the opportunity to do more," says Koch. "Sticking to that seemingly simple rule isn't always simple, but it is always worth it."

During the day-to-day madness, with the phone ringing and e-mails piling up, it is easy to lose clarity of vision. To maintain focus, many creatives are thinking outside the

box—trying everything from team-building exercises, group sketchbooks, and show-and-tell to group challenges, field trips, and mobilized meetings, where business is conducted during the course of a brisk walk. "Every quarter, we go away overnight as a group to examine our business practices, talk about future goals, and examine where we want to be," says Sheree Clark of Sayles Graphic Design. "The agenda changes every time. If we have a new staff person, we will do some team assimilation of that person into our corporate culture. If we have run into a lot of production snags, we will sit down and talk about our processes and see what we need to do to tighten them up. As a result, we are closer as a group." Ric Riordon of the Riordon Design Group adds, "We want to make sure our designers are continuing to look and to be inspired. So we use a sketchbook as a creative catalyst within the studio. Every day, somebody adds something to it—a sketch, poetry, or prose. They look during the week for something that inspires them. When that sketchbook lands on their desk, it gets fed."

In a highly competitive marketplace that speaks to reduced budgets, creatives must, more than ever, set themselves apart from the competition. Rethinking one's brand and identity from the inside out requires brutal honesty, intensive evaluation, and commitment. For those willing to embrace the challenges rather than being threatened by them, prosperity will yield growth and renewal.

creating distinction

Wow! A Branding Company specializes in developing innovative practices geared toward helping companies understand, implement, and manage their brand. When it came time to establish their own identity and business system, Wow! put their time-proven process to work. "A lot of people start with a logo and try to work everything around that," says creative director Dann Ilicic. "We call the logo the punctuation to the identity, not the identity."

For their business card, Wow! began by setting all existing assumptions aside to reexamine form, function, and its relevance in today's business world. "The things that we questioned were why business cards are made out of paper, why they are typically 2 by 3 ½ inches (5 by 9 centimeter), and why they need to fit inside a Rolodex when everyone uses some form of electronic organizer," details Ilicic. "The ultimate function of a business card is to create an impression, so we pushed the design team to start looking for alternatives." In search of something distinctive, they explored materials from rubber and plastic to metal. A stainless steel surface was the clear winner.

To transform the metallic surface into a functional card, the design team looked at a variety of techniques before deciding on laser cutting. "It was difficult in the beginning because we really didn't know what we were asking for," recalls Ilicic. "It took a few months to figure out just how to do it." The metallic cards were laser-cut from a 4- by 8-foot (1.2- by 2.4-meter) sheet of stainless steel, leaving a slight tab around each card for silk-screen

printing purposes. To smooth the rough edges, a process called tumbling was employed. This had a dulling effect on the surface, so a varnish was later sprayed on top to bring back luster and protect the silk-screen-printed type from scratching off.

To complete their stationery package, Wow! developed letterhead with an unconventional horizontal orientation—a reflection of today's digital letter-writing preference. Rather than standard #10 envelopes, the branding firm chose silver antistatic bags that were blind embossed with the company's logo. By questioning traditional practices and venturing outside the norm, Wow! was able to develop an identity system that stood out from the competition. "Whenever anyone asks for our card, it is hard not to smile because we know the reaction we are going to get," says Ilicic. "We find that when we go to net-working events and functions, the cards always end up traveling throughout the room."

If you present the marketplace with nothing unique, you open yourself up to becoming a sophisticated order taker, leaving the opportunity for buyers to price-shop alternatives.

FIRM: WOW! A BRANDING COMPANY

CREATIVE DIRECTOR: DANN ILICIC

DESIGNER: PERRY CHUA

PRINTING: SPECIAL SCREENCRAFT PRINTING (CARD)

SPECIAL TECHNIQUES AND MANUFACTURER:

INDUSTRIAL LASER CUTTING (METAL)

Being selective in your approach to new business is key. By developing relationships with clients who share your vision, you begin to build recognition and market value.

choosing the right projects

It is important to be selective about the projects you choose to work on, as they can dictate the type of work that will come in the future. Although this brochure was designed to raise awareness for Mat Wright as a photographer, it was also a great demonstration of Origin's capabilities as a design company. "We use this piece as a promotional item to reflect our philosophy, level of craft, and attention to detail," explains creative director and designer Mark Bottomley.

To drive the messaging of the piece, the designer came up with the theme of talking pictures. "Mat is a great portrait photographer and also a very no-nonsense person. He doesn't dress his work up with fancy words or explanations. He just takes great pictures," says Bottomley. "It's quite simple. The pictures just speak for themselves." Because the work didn't need any commentary for it to communicate to its audience, the piece became a picture book. To deliver just the right look and feel, the designer researched paper and bindery options for materials that would complement Wright's dramatic photographic style. To create the front and back covers, Curtis Malts Spirit 100-gram uncoated stock was adhered over 3-millimeter gray board. Both pieces were bound to a Curtis Malts Islay 300-gram inner cover, leaving a large silk-screen-printed spine showing on the left-hand side. Saddle stitching was used to bind the inside pages to the inner cover. Overall, the promotion boasted a distinctive and innovative presentation.

To protect and add the final finishing touch to the photographic picture book, a matching slipcase was created. "The activity of pulling the book out makes the viewer feel the paper and really appreciate the piece as a whole," adds the designer. "It also gives the book a much greater impact overall." By being selective in their approach to new business, Origin was able to add to their portfolio with work that really showcases their creative abilities.

CLIENT: MAT WRIGHT PHOTOGRAPHY

FIRM: ORIGIN

CREATIVE DIRECTOR AND DESIGNER:
MARK BOTTOMLEY

PHOTOGRAPHY: MAT WRIGHT

PRINTING AND BINDERY: APS GROUP

practicing what you preach

The fun, diverse, and eclectic group at Brown & Company Design has found creative and inventive ways in which to express their personality in almost everything they do, from the way they pitch clients to how they conduct day-to-day business. "Our marketing and new business area, a room with a big glass window that we call the fishbowl, has a funky leather couch, hanging bikes, a vintage barber chair, an Elvis jumpsuit for special occasions, and gumball machines filled with goodies for clients to snack on while they wait. Having all this in the entrance is purposeful, as it helps to set expectations," shares creative director and designer Chris Lamy. "We also have vintage days, cowboy days, and disco days where we all dress appropriately and carry on business as usual. We've even built a life-size robot suit once to deliver a proposal to a toy company. Our clients respect our thought process, and the work that comes in from them reflects that." When it came to providing visiting clientele with directions to their office, Brown & Company Design was not shy about flexing their creative muscle. Instead of merely giving details over the phone or sending a PDF map, the ingenious firm chose to build a three-dimensional virtual experience, making the trip to their firm memorable.

To serve as visual reference when a client was en route, members of the creative team cleverly photographed each other at various landmarks and highway exit signs. Each developed image was then placed in its appropriate position inside a View-Master reel. For the last image, the entire company was featured holding letters that spelled out the incoming client's name in 3-D. "It help set the tone for what the client could expect once they set foot inside the building," says Lamy. "It also let them know that we were a fun and creative firm." Because Brown & Company Design used their staff in all of the shots, clients saw familiar faces once they arrived.

To achieve the 3-D look, a Fisher-Price View-Master was used. The camera creates the illusion of three-dimensional space by taking two pictures simultaneously from a dual lens. "The patented View-Master cutter punches matching sets of slides out to a specific shape, allowing them to go into the reel in only one direction," Lamy explains. "All you need to do is ask the developer not to cut and mount the slides in frames." If you do not want to purchase the necessary equipment, companies like View-Master will not only rent out 3-D cameras but will also put your slides into reels.

To house the View-Master and reel, the team developed an engaging retro-style package. "We wanted the piece to stand out from the clutter on a prospect's desk," offers Lamy. "We also wanted it to look like a toy, something fun." Each box and insert was printed on heavy card stock and hand-cut, scored, and assembled in-house. The accent photography, taken during one of the firm's well-known theme days, featured the staff wearing 1950s-style vintage clothing. A small booklet, providing a hard copy of the directions and a phone number, was also included so the incoming client wouldn't have to keep looking through the View-Master while driving. The overall package and idea was entertaining and engaging, helping set a positive tone for incoming clients.

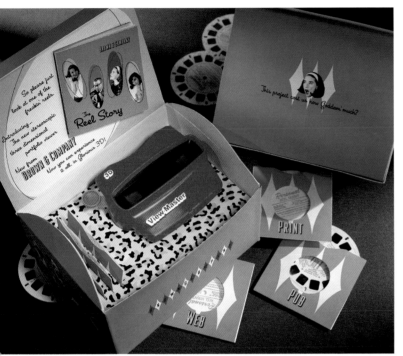

FIRM: BROWN & COMPANY DESIGN

CREATIVE DIRECTORS AND DESIGNERS:
MARY JO BROWN AND CHRIS LAMY

PRODUCTION AND ILLUSTRATION: CHRIS HAMER

PHOTOGRAPHY: CLAUDIA KAERNER AND MARY JO BROWN

PRINTING: ON DEMAND IMAGING

SPECIAL TECHNIQUES: HOVEYS (FILM OUTPUT)

MANUFACTURERS: FISHER-PRICE (VIEW-MASTER),
REEL 3-D ENTERPRISES (REEL MOUNTS)

To survive in today's marketplace, you need to establish what makes you different from the competition. By defining your niche, you are setting a foundation on which to strategically position and build your brand.

"We are trying to position ourselves not only as the design firm that offers high-quality services but also as the one that provides unexpected solutions and concepts," says creative director and designer Nedjeljko Spoljar. "We wanted to create a piece that would reflect our ability to explore and use new techniques and to put things in unusual contexts." While making freeform notations in a sketchbook, the designer made an interesting discovery. "I realized that the sentence 'We love you' could be expanded to 'We love your money' simply by adding one letter and another word," observes Spoljar. "The combination makes a funny, surprising, and unusual statement." The next step was to find an interesting and innovative way in which to present the concept. "I had been waiting for a chance to use the scratch technique on something for a long time, and it was a perfect solution for this particular problem," Spoljar adds.

Taking their inspiration from scratch-off game cards, the design firm took their idea to Printel, one of the best printing houses in their area. The biggest challenge for both the printer and design firm came in trying to find just the right combination of paper and scratch-off ink to make the concept work. The ink not only had to scratch off easily but also had to be opaque enough so the type did not show through. "Because I wanted to create a great contrast between the paper texture and the smooth scratch surface, I tried to use a beautiful uncoated paper called Conqueror CX22. It was a disastrous solution because the ink couldn't be scratched off at all," acknowledges Spoljar. "Then I tried again using Sappi Magnomatt paper. It has a very fine and smooth coating that kept the ink on the surface, enabling it to be scratched." The process turned out to be quite simple in the end. First the cards were offset-printed in one color: black. The scratch-off substance, silver metallic ink mixed with glue, was then silk-screened onto the printed sheets. "The glue keeps the ink elastic to enable scratching, and the silk-screen color makes the ink nontransparent," notes Spoljar. After the cards were thoroughly dried, they were trimmed to the designer's specifications.

The layout was kept simple in order to call attention to the overall concept. "From our friends and peers to the marketing directors and museum curators that we work with, the cards seem to be interesting to anyone who gets them," concludes Spoljar. "We're planning to produce more materials using the same technique." Sensus Design Factory was able to highlight their unconventional idea with a familiar but not widely used technique, giving life and interest to an otherwise traditional card. The resulting work attracted international attention not only from the design community but also from prospective and existing clients.

TECHNICAL TIPS

If you are interested in using a scratch-off technique, do not attempt the process on an uncoated paper because it will not work. If you are adamant about using uncoated paper, try applying a varnish or lamination to the area on which the scratch-off coating will be applied. To avoid all potential problems, however, a smooth coated surface works best.

1

The studio name and contact information is offset-printed onto a coated white stock. The scratchable ink is then silk-screen printed in silver on top, leaving only the company name showing. The recipient has to actively scratch off the silver to see the contact information underneath.

2

The back of the card features a tricky play with words. At first glance, a sentence reads "We love you," but as the surface is scratched, an entirely different message is revealed.

1
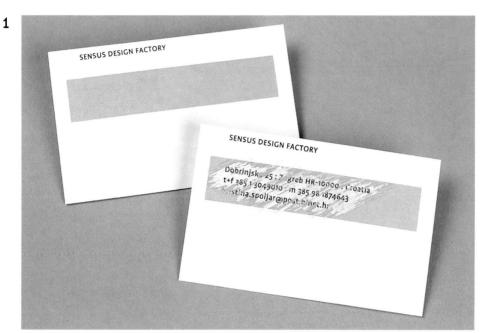

FIRM: SENSUS DESIGN FACTORY

CREATIVE DIRECTOR AND DESIGNER:
NEDJELJKO SPOLJAR

PRINTING: PRINTEL D.O.O.

SPECIAL TECHNIQUES:
PRINTEL D.O.O. (SCRATCH-OFF MATERIAL)

2

fun and stylish

The three-panel letter-folded invitation uses custom die-cut angles to simulate the walls and windows of the design studio. It is printed in four PMS colors and an overall matte varnish for a flat, solid look. It was sent in a semi-transparent envelope with a custom die-cut label to existing and prospective clients as well as vendors.

For Kolégramdesign's tenth anniversary, the creative team wanted to celebrate by having a happening cocktail party, retro style. "We think of ourselves as fun people, and we wanted to portray that in our promotion," admits designer Gontran Blais. "We also wanted to create something that people would remember, use, and relate to." The only challenge was developing an event that everyone in the studio was happy with. "We had a big brainstorming session, and almost everyone had a different concept," recalls Blais. "It is really hard when you are doing work for yourself and you have to please everyone." In the end, the team agreed that a fun and stylish yet classy promotion was the way to go.

The design team began with the invitation. "Because the party was to be held at our studio, we wanted the invitation to reflect the walls and windows of our space," says Blais. The invitation featured die-cut angles in a three-panel letter-fold format, thus conveying the sense of perspective and three-dimensional space the design team was looking for. They liked the angular architecture of the invitation so much they decided to carry the look through the entire promotion and event.

At the custom-decorated celebration, a barmaid served cocktails in martini glasses to guests ; a DJ played music throughout the night. As a parting gift, each guest was given a bar accessory kit. The package included a set of four tin coasters, a minibooklet of drink recipes, and a notebook for jotting down choice mixers. The coasters, which came standard in a tin box, were silk-screen-printed with an epoxy-based ink in five colors, including a double hit of white. Because of the beveled edge, the coasters could not be printed with a full bleed, as initially intended. The words *funky, groovy, wow,* and *cool* work hand-in-hand with the graphics to carry forward the retro theme that started with the invitation. The elongated shape of the booklet of drink recipes, the staff's personal mixers, was a nice addition to the overall square presentation. To ensure the tin box and notebook stayed together as a unit, a custom sleeve was designed to fit snugly around both items so neither would slide out. A secondary wrap was also created to completely seal the contents. "With the kit, there is one surprise after the other," concludes Blais. "People actually had a Christmas face when they opened it." Because the firm maintained a consistent look and theme, the resulting event and promotion were successful.

TECHNICAL TIPS

When you are working on an event, consider the whole package as a series of related parts. To maintain cohesion, begin with a theme and work on every aspect at once. Limit the ink coverage on tin surfaces and allow the color of the surface work for you. This will keep costs down and minimize noticeable surface scratches. Epoxy-based ink adheres best to metal surfaces.

The parting gift consisted of a set of silk-screen-printed tin coasters, a perfect-bound notebook, and a custom die-cut recipe book for drinks. A custom wrap holds them firmly together in a nice package. All of the pieces contain the same flat colors and angular retro theme that was initiated in the first point of contact—the invitation.

The Flash-animated screensaver, used on every screen at the party, reinforces the custom graphics and the overall retro theme.

1

3

2

FIRM: KOLÉGRAMDESIGN

CREATIVE DIRECTOR: ANNIE TANGUAY

ART DIRECTOR: MIKE TEIXEIRA

DESIGNER: GONTRAN BLAIS

PRINTING: IMPRIMERIE DU PROGRÈS (INVITATION) AND SÉRIGRAPHIE ALBION (COASTERS)

BINDERY: IMPRIMERIE DU PROGRÈS (NOTEBOOK)

SPECIAL TECHNIQUES: CAPITAL BOX (DIE-CUTTING)

MANUFACTURER: BRYMARK PROMOTIONS (TIN BOX AND COASTERS)

simple but
meaningful

Hartpappe (1 millimeter), a bookmaking material, was the stock of choice. Its black-and-gray camouflage look, which came standard, intrigued the design team because of its military connotations. The piece is entitled *Wahrnehmungsgerät*, which means "perception tool." Typ 21/7-klein was added at the end to give the piece a mechanical context. A small tag with the MAGMA logo on the back is attached to voice the firm's political opinion about war.

"Every year we send out something from our office to friends and clients," says art director Lars Harmsen. "After September 11th, we really didn't feel like having something big, expensive, and obviously self-promotional to send out. It was a time to look at things from a different angle." Wanting to refocus people's attention, MAGMA developed an interesting tool they call Wahrnehmungsgerät typ 21/7-klein. In German, *Wahrnehmung* means "perception" and *Gerät* means "tool." "It is a perception tool to see the smaller things of this world, reducing things to what is really important," explains Harmsen. "It is a small piece that has a lot of political meaning for us." The 21/7-klein was added to the name for a mechanical touch, similar to how one refers to an engine of a car. This "engine to see things," as coined by Harmsen, is quite simple but very meaningful in a time when many people are feeling introspective.

Designed to crop out distraction, the perception tool forces people to narrow their focus and look within their own communities to see how they can make a difference. The grommet hole and rounded edges of the device help highlight the firm's logo, an oil tower. "The idea behind our logo is to say that our research is done very deeply and our work is very rich—tearing out of the ground," offers Harmsen.

The piece sits nicely inside an orange slip holder. The semicircle die-cuts that adorn each side make the piece easy to access. The text and graphics that provide operating instructions to the viewer are not offset printed but photocopied onto Colorit by Schneidersöhne. "To offset print was not necessary. It is not important to have things printed in fancy ways," says Harmsen. "It is the idea that counts." In a palette of orange, silver, and black, the ingenious device is an innovative way to communicate the firm's beliefs and philosophies.

"There are two different categories of promotion," concludes Harmsen. "There is one that uses a brochure to show off past work. Then you have another approach where the dialog is much more intelligent. It is more of an idea or visualization of how your agency behaves or sees things. In my opinion, the latter is a more communicative approach." The promotion was delivered in the firm's corporate stationery.

TECHNICAL TIPS

To create an extraordinary, intelligent promotion, you have to make the idea your number-one priority. Spend time researching and develop an approach that is neither typical nor mainstream. Encourage vendors to keep you updated on new surfaces and techniques. If you can find custom-looking materials that come standard, you will save time and money by not having to print or produce them.

| 2 | 3 |

The company logo is stamped in silver foil on the back, providing an interesting contrast to the matte surface. The orange holder, photocopied in black, describes how to operate the perception tool.

The intriguing little device is sent to clients, vendors, friends, and colleagues using the design firm's stationery. MAGMA's corporate identity—graphic images of volcanoes and oil towers in a palette of orange, silver, and black—is carried through the distinctive series of business cards and letterhead.

2

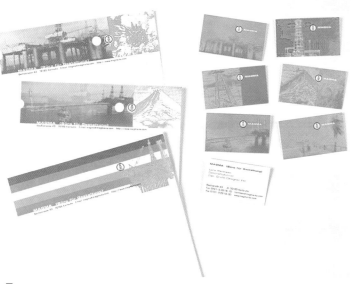

1

3

FIRM: MAGMA [BÜRO FÜR GESTALTUNG]

ART DIRECTORS: LARS HARMSEN AND ULRICH WEIß

DESIGNER: ULRICH WEIß

SPECIAL TECHNIQUES: BUCHBINDER MEISTER LUDWIG WEISS

the little engine that could

After completing a challenging series of high-profile full-color ads for the Pharmaceutical Researchers and Manufacturers of America (PhRMA), Grafik knew their heroic feat was worth tooting their whistle about. "In a very short period, we had designed fifteen ads for a single issue of *Newsweek*," recalls creative director and designer David Collins. "We were trying to break into the pharmaceutical market and felt our experience with PhRMA would help us in working with other pharmaceutical companies. The idea was to tell our story to the industry."

Grafik put on their thinking caps and thought of an interesting and captivating way to tell their story. "We bounced around a lot of ideas, knowing that we needed to grab the attention of the target audience—pharmaceutical marketing executives," Collins details. "Because we are a small company, compared to the much larger agencies that do most of the pharmaceutical advertising, we felt that the *Little Engine That Could* was an appropriate metaphor." To deliver the message, the design team chose a wooden train whistle. Its interesting shape and instant appeal made it the perfect vehicle. "The train whistle is a gimmick, but it relates to a very powerful story," reminds Collins.

To bring life to their concept, Grafik researched a variety of options, looking for the one that provided just the right look and feel. "We found a vendor that produced wooden train whistles in various sizes," notes Collins, "and would literally brand any message into the side within a limited space." To imprint type and graphics on both sides of the whistle, the firm had to provided the vendor with a digital file. They also made a prototype prior to final production to ensure the product was what they envisioned.

To complete the package, a brochure featuring the emotionally charged series of ads was wrapped around the whistle and the two were placed inside a box with packing material that simulated wood shavings. Grafik labeled the box with a visually arresting teaser, enticing the recipient to look inside. "Once the recipient gets into the mailer, all fifteen ads are clearly presented along with a brief case study," adds Collins. "Because there is no way to tell the complete story, we determined that the audience should have the option to see more. To accomplish this, our call to action was a Web page designed to give more detail about the ad campaign and provide access to the rest of the Grafik site." The story-driven mailer helped position Grafik as a small agency that generates big results for their clients.

TECHNICAL TIPS

To attract attention, don't give away the entire story; leave the audience wanting more—and always have a follow-up procedure in place to capitalize on your efforts. When imprinting into wood, make sure the level of detail and impact are what you want by having a prototype made first.

The elongated box shape and the intriguing teaser spark interest and curiosity. Inside, a wooden whistle is wrapped with the tagline "Forget I think I can. This red-hot engine did," making a connection between Grafik's efforts and a powerful childhood story.

The whistle is imprinted with the firm's identity on one side and their Web site on the other. The URL www.grafik.com/justwhistle provides information about the case study that could not be detailed in the direct mailer. It also introduces interested parties to the rest of Grafik's work and experience. The minibrochure that wraps the whistle includes all fifteen ads that ran in a single issue of *Newsweek*.

1

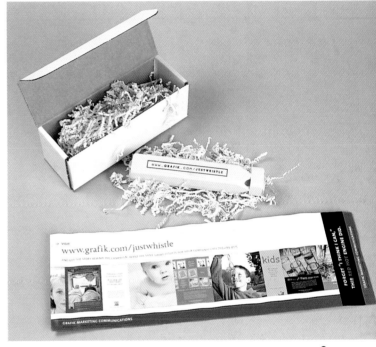

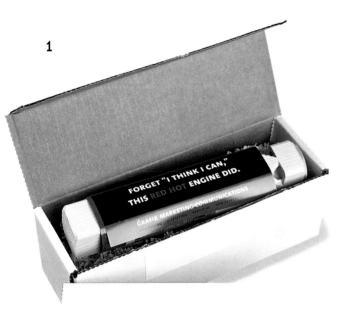

2

FIRM: GRAFIK

CREATIVE DIRECTOR: DAVID COLLINS

DESIGNERS: JONATHAN AMEN, DAVID COLLINS, AND RON HARMON

PRINTING: COLORCRAFT OF VIRGINIA, INC.

SPECIAL TECHNIQUES: SPECIALTIES, INC. (WOOD BRANDING)

MANUFACTURERS: SPECIALTIES, INC. (TRAIN WHISTLE), ULINE (BOX), AND PAPER MART (PACKING MATERIAL)

sporting style

The 2002 fashion season was underway, and Reebok needed to draw attention to their new line. "We wanted to get into the minds of fashion and celebrity stylists to encourage them to use our products when styling a TV show, movie, or fashion layout," explains creative director and designer Eleni Chronopoulos. "Given that they are creative people, we thought a uniquely shaped sketchbook made of interesting materials would be appealing, something they would certainly want to hold onto."

With the desire to incorporate unconventional materials and techniques in her design, Chronopoulos consulted production experts for assistance. "I worked with our materials manager to explore material and branding options for the cover and a production expert to figure out how to put the whole thing together," she details. After exploring a variety of options, the designer chose embossed red synthetic leather as an exciting way to set the stage for the modish piece. The surface was not only highly tactile but also representative of Reebok's fashion sense. The biggest problem was that the material, produced by the roll in Asia, was available in a diagonal pattern only. "We needed it to run vertically," acknowledges Chronopoulos. "This meant each piece had to be carefully lined up before cutting. Not only did it produce a lot of waste, it also slowed down the process." Once the synthetic material was correctly cut to the designer's specifications, it was mounted onto an 80-lb. black cover stock to give it substance and support. As an accent, a two-color stamped-aluminum logo, an existing detail in Reebok's apparel, was adhered to the cover with rivets.

The inside pages included an attractive array of fun and fashionable footwear and apparel intermixed with open pages available for sketching and creative notation of potential ways in which to use the new line. To add further interest, the piece was bound with custom rivets. Using materials and detailing from key footwear and apparel pieces helped Reebok give the audience a tactile glimpse into what the product line had to offer. "We could have easily sent a postcard to anyone remotely related to the entertainment industry," shares Chronopoulos, "but we knew we would have more of an impact targeting the influencers, in this case stylists, with a more thoughtful piece." It was sent in a black rope-tie envelope accented with a custom label. The only point of contact was a nick die-cut Rolodex card.

TECHNICAL TIPS

When using thin or highly flexible material as a cover, it is best to mount it to a rigid surface to add stability and strength. Look to other industries, like fashion, to find materials and accents that are available standard but look custom-made in a design context. Never be afraid to consult with specialists about alternative materials and techniques. They can make the experience a painless one.

1 | **2**

The brochure's cover, made of red synthetic leather and accented by a two-color aluminum tag, is both fashionable and sporty. The piece is sent to stylists in a black rope-tie envelope.

Inside, Reebok's 2002 seasonal line is displayed. To make the piece useful to stylists, blank pages for sketching and notation are added. Each page is perforated, allowing it to be easily ripped out of the book and used. A nick die-cut Rolodex card is the only point of contact.

FIRM: REEBOK DESIGN SERVICES

CREATIVE DIRECTOR AND DESIGNER:

ELENI CHRONOPOULOS

PHOTOGRAPHY: GARY LAND

PRINTING AND BINDERY: ATLAS PRESS, INC.

MANUFACTURERS: PAPER ACCESS (ENVELOPES) AND REEBOK

INTERNATIONAL LTD. (SYNTHETIC LEATHER AND ALUMINUM TAG)

2

1

defining
the edge

The departments of landscape architecture and urban planning and design at Harvard Design School undertook a joint venture that focused on Hong Kong's waterfront. Twelve students and two professors traveled to the harborside city to examine issues of density, connectivity, and sustainability. Upon completion of the educational endeavor, the university wanted to document their findings in a unique way that would not only capture the essence of the city but also appeal to architectural and urban designers, policy makers, city officials and planners, and the general public at large. The creative team of Nassar Design was up for the challenge.

To get a solid understanding of the city, the studio experience, and the work that was generated, the design team attended both the midterm and final reviews in Hong Kong. "This enabled us to provide the client with an overall design strategy and production budget," adds creative director and designer Nelida Nassar. "From there, preliminary sketches were drawn and different book trim sizes were tested." Because of the monumental quality of the architectural structures involved, a vertical format was chosen. The perfect-bound book was divided into two main areas of interest: commencing with an analytical section and closing with a more visual presentation. "Several thumbnails utilizing different grids and page layouts were studied," notes Nassar. In the end, a simple two-column structure was chosen. Throughout the educational publication, striking imperial red-and-gold duotones are juxtaposed with informative essays and groundbreaking research.

To make the piece stand out and have the unique quality the university was looking for, the design team did considerable research, looking through their archives, consulting the Web, and searching specialty stores for new and innovative products. "We really wanted to use a new material to express the energy of the city of Hong Kong," shares Nassar. The search paid off when they located the perfect surface for the book's cover; a lenticular film, which gives a three-dimensional feel to a two-dimensional surface, was chosen for its highly reflective surface and grid pattern. "The design was influenced by both the fluctuating lights, typical of harbor cities, and the more down-to-earth urban grid and physical configuration of the city's form," details Nassar. To add stability and strength, the lenticular material was laminated to a coated cover stock.

As part of the book's title, the words *Defining the Edge* also offered an opportunity for innovation. As a finishing touch, the type was set along the outer trim using a striking yellow foil stamp that calls attention to the edge and frames the highly reflective grid pattern inside. The resulting publication was not only stunning and dramatic but also served as an invaluable resource for students, educators, and professionals.

TECHNICAL TIPS

Purchase lenticular paper in sheets rather than in rolls, as sheets allow better control and eliminate unwanted curling. Be sure to order the sheets without an adhesive backing if you plan to laminate them to another surface. To imprint a lenticular sheet, foil stamping seems to offer both an opaque look and strong adhesion. Other processes, like silk-screen and offset, can cause registration problems when printing onto the outer trim.

1

The highly reflective and geometric cover, made of a lenticular film mounted on to a 10-point Kromekote board, helps communicate Hong Kong's urban grid and the flickering lights of its illuminated harbor. The typographic treatment, imprinted using foil stamping with a special mix yellow, was set along the trim to call attention to the book's title, *Hong Kong: Defining the Edge*.

2

The interior begins with a synopsis by various historians and urban design specialists. This is followed by a visual presentation of the work produced by the student participants. The book is distributed to architectural and urban design students, professors, and professionals as well as to policy makers, city officials and planners, and the general public.

1

2

CLIENT: HARVARD DESIGN SCHOOL

FIRM: NASSAR DESIGN

CREATIVE DIRECTOR: NELIDA NASSAR

DESIGNERS: NELIDA NASSAR AND MARGARITA ENCOMIENDA

ILLUSTRATION AND PHOTOGRAPHY: HARVARD DESIGN SCHOOL

PRINTING: MERRILL/DANIELS

BINDERY: CREATIVE FINISHINGS, INC.

MANUFACTURER: COBURN CORPORATION (LENTICULAR PAPER)

unique

chapter two:

construc-
tions,

folds,

and die-

cuts

The architecture of the promotional brochure is evolving, and creatives are thinking outside the box when it comes to format and construction. From custom-molded containers and hand-made boxes to multipieced assemblages, pop-ups, and animated flipbooks, today's promotions are putting a new face on the once typical brochure. Unique constructions captivate an audience with their engaging folds, clever inserts, and interesting die-cut shapes. The interaction encourages active participation, and the overall messaging becomes memorable.

"When you encourage exploration, it starts to feed a lot of different venues," admits Dan Wheaton of the Riordon Design Group, Inc. "For instance, the engineering of a box to function in more than one capacity is not only innovative but also a way of exposing clients to different possibilities." To extend the life and effectiveness of any promotion, it is advantageous to consider creating a piece that can also be functional, acting as a keepsake or novelty item on someone's desk. That way, when it is time to assign a project, your firm comes to mind. If your promotion contains nothing for the recipients, they have no reason to hang on to it.

When developing promotions, don't be afraid to employ the assistance of professionals outside the communications industry. For instance, the assistance of an industrial designer helped to make DSM's watering container a beautiful interlacing of form and function, and an origami expert put an interesting twist on Weidlinger Associates' fiftieth anniversary promotion. Outside specialists have the knowledge and expertise that can raise any promotional endeavor to a high level of distinction.

shelter of dreams

A miniature keepsake, built in the spirit of the Red Canoe cabin, is given as a heartfelt gift to clients, colleagues, and friends. It is sent along with a special note, encouraging recipients to use it as a source of inspiration and a shelter for their dreams. It is hand-signed by the Canoeists, a title that the partners at Red Canoe have come to love.

Four years ago, Caroline Kavanagh and Deb Koch forged into the woods to build a partnership in a place where they could live and work in harmony with nature. A cabin amid 350 acres of breathtaking wilderness became their safe haven and their muse. After celebrating yet another successful year in business, the partners at Red Canoe began to reflect, reexamining what started them on such a wondrous journey. In an attempt to share their shelter of dreams with others, the partners embarked on the construction of miniature cabins—representatives of the sanctuary that has brought the collaborators joy over the last four years. The individually hand-crafted labors of love serve as a home for inspirational notes, pictures, or the special cards one receives. The dimensions are 8 (wide) by 11 ½ (long) by 10 ½-inch (tall).

Many of the cabins' special details and accents originate from the breathtaking beauty of the great outdoors that surround the peaceful respite known as Red Canoe. Wood, sticks, and river rock that make the cabin come alive were collected as bits of tranquility to be shared. In building the keepsake pieces, the creative team looked toward the original construction of their Red Canoe cabin for guidance. "The interior walls of our cabin are made of rough-cut pine. The little cabins use squared logs of that same wood," details Kavanagh. "Here our ceilings and floors are birch, and the roofs and windows on the little cabins use that same birch." Because of the cabins' miniature scale, working tools had to be adapted to fit each task. For instance, a nail gun was vital, as the size and delicacy of the piece didn't allow for hammering. Clothespins worked perfectly as little clamps to assist in securely adhering the twigs with wood glue to the rooftops. The canoe that rests on the side of the cabin and the paddles that accent the door were both hand-whittled. To make the chimney, flat river stones were adhered with cedar-colored caulking. As a finishing treatment, each cabin was checked for sharp edges, which were filed down if necessary. The only point of contact was a subtle silk-screen printing of the company's contact information and original mission statement: *As we live, so we work.*

Each cabin was carefully wrapped and tied with twine. A poetic note, detailing the intent of the keepsake promotion, was attached. The piece was sent in a cardboard box wrapped with custom-designed packing paper created especially for the promotion. The care and love for one's craft expressed by the canoe workers featured on the outer wrapping resonated with the partners at Red Canoe, who felt compelled to preserve these ideas. Each of the 150 signed-and-numbered limited-edition pieces of art was sent to clients and special people who had become a part of the Red Canoe family over the years. The heartfelt gift was a way to show appreciation and gratitude for the wonderful experiences that have been shared.

TECHNICAL TIPS

With a project of this type, make a model to act as a guide. After establishing the final specifications from the prototype, it is helpful to have every item in sample form for sizing purposes. If you plan on doing the handwork yourself, make sure you will enjoy the process, as you will be a very unhappy camper otherwise. Producing a labor-intensive promotion such as this one involves much trial and error. You must be resourceful in choosing materials and processes. If you are up for the challenge, you must be mindful of the big picture, and don't get too focused on the minute details. Allow time for the complications that may arise. Note that wood must be very smooth to receive a silk-screen-printed message legibly.

DO IT FOR LESS

To save money, search for an off-the-shelf alternative and adapt it accordingly. This approach would, however, greatly diminish the piece's authenticity and uniqueness, which are such big parts of the concept.

2

One can enter the cabin's sanctuary by either lifting the roof or unlocking the door to the secret attic space upstairs—a place for little treasures, inspirational notes, and personal pictures. Once inside, one is presented with Red Canoe's contact information and philosophical tagline: *As we live, so we work.* Each cabin is a handcrafted, limited-edition piece of art.

The cabin is wrapped with twine and accented by a poetic note. Each signature piece is placed inside a box wrapped with custom packing paper created specifically for the promotion. The archival photography features early Canadian canoe factories and their dedicated workers.

As a follow-up, another promotion was sent four months later. Created as an April Fool's Day joke, the promotion alerts recipients to their cabin's flawed chimney flue. The notice—complete with illustrated diagrams, step-by-step instructions, and a recall form—seems quite legitimate and fooled many of its recipients. But after careful inspection and a trip to the dedicated Web site(www.redcanoe.com/flueproof), one came away with quite a chuckle. The clever promotion was sent in a box perfectly sized to fit the chimney, including protective bubble wrap. The piece became a reminder of how little time we take from our busy lives to really look at and appreciate the simplest things. The cabin and its follow-up were meant to give recipients renewed respect and appreciation for the God-given gifts we all share.

1

FIRM: RED CANOE

CREATIVE DIRECTORS AND DESIGNERS:
    DEB KOCH AND CAROLINE KAVANAGH

ILLUSTRATION: CAROLINE KAVANAGH

PHOTOGRAPHY: NATIONAL ARCHIVES OF CANADA AND
    PROVINCIAL ARCHIVES OF NEW BRUNSWICK (WRAPPING PAPER)

PRINTING: LITHOGRAPHICS, INC. (WRAPPING PAPER),
    STUDIO INK (SILK-SCREEN PRINTING), AND EPSON INKJET
    (NOTE AND TRIFOLD RECALL NOTICE)

SPECIAL TECHNIQUES: DEB KOCH, CAROLINE KAVANAGH,
    MARTHA AUTHEMENT, MORGAN AUTHEMENT,
    AND SONJA USRY (MASONRY)

MANUFACTURERS: NICK WARNER (CARPENTRY), TALLENT PLANNING
    & LUMBER (PINE WOOD), LOWES (HINGES, CAULKING, AND PAINT), ULINE
    (BOX, PACKING PAPER, AND TWINE), SHAKER WORKSHOPS (PAINT FOR
    CANOE), RED CANOE SITE (TWIGS FOR WINDOW AND ROOF TRIM AND STONES
    FOR CHIMNEY)

3

4

dreams for a better world

The custom-designed watering can is made out of polypropylene 5 (PP5). It houses a creativity book, inspirational video, and packet of seeds.

DSM was having their one-hundreth anniversary and wanted to do something monumental to celebrate. "They were looking for us to create a special gift for their employees," recalls creative director and designer Hans Wolbers. "The philosophy of the company is all about the word *unlimited*, which stands for unlimited possibilities in research. So we used their mission to implement and create this idea." Through the project, employees from around the world were invited to make a positive contribution to the planet by putting forth their dreams and talents. The project was delivered in the form of a contest where the best ideas would be realized.

To serve as mentors, the design team went in search of people that have put their dreams into action, making a difference in the world as a result. A diverse group of people with social and environmental pursuits was chosen. "We wanted to inspire all the employees and let them know that it is not so difficult to realize their personal dreams," says Wolbers. To get the employees' creative juices flowing, the design team employed the theories of Dr. Edward de Bono, "He is a famous professor who did research on how creativity works," offers Wolbers. "I went to a couple of his workshops and became really inspired. When this project came along, I decided to use his ideas." Throughout the promotional book, de Bono's theories are presented in an interactive fashion. Random stimulation, reuse, and opportunity seeking were chosen for their ability to change attitudes and fixed perceptions.

As a working tool for participating employees around the world to begin their journey, a spiral-bound creativity book was developed in several languages. "We wanted the book to be something you take out every day and read, draw in, and discover new details," adds Wolbers. The book and a companion video served as vehicles to inspire and enlighten the employees of DSM to participate in the once-in-a-lifetime opportunity. As a finishing touch, a packet of seeds was included in the ensemble as a symbol of growth and renewal. The book, video, and seeds were housed inside a custom-designed plastic watering can. The entire project, inspirational and uplifting, was a way for DSM to promote their friendly face to the world. It was launched at a worldwide breakfast for all the employees.

TECHNICAL TIPS

Lenticular printing, which creates the illusion of three-dimensional space and motion, comprises a flat image that is either mounted or printed directly on a lenticular lens material. If you are interested in utilizing this technique, consult a company that specializes in the process to see all of the animation options available.

To create innovative, multifunctional packaging, don't be afraid to employ the assistance of industrial designers, who understand how to manipulate materials and have readily available lists of necessary suppliers to make it happen.

With worldwide distribution, many organizational details must be attended to. First and foremost, the project must be translated in a way that is sensitive and knowledgeable about each language and culture. Outside experts are vital to assist in this process. If you are interested in distributing seeds internationally, geographic climates and custom importing regulations must be investigated thoroughly for each country. It would be counterproductive to send seeds for a tree that does not grow in a specific area or to have packages held up in customs. To ensure the right book, video, and seeds find their way to the appropriate country, an organizational plan must be put in place and a team assigned to the task.

DO IT FOR LESS

The custom-molded watering can could be replaced with a prefabricated outer packaging. You could also limit the inks and paper selection to one source for the booklet.

The spiral-bound book and video are tools used
to inspire and enlighten the employees of DSM.
The animation graphics that introduce the
video also appear on the cover of the book as
a three-dimensional lenticular sticker. The
seeds, symbolizing growth, and the use of
recycled and wood-free paper help spread a
positive message about respecting and giving
back to the environment. A hand-lettered card
introduces the concept in a personalized and
uplifting way. Both the book and video are
produced in Dutch, English, French, German,
Italian, Portuguese, and Spanish.

The book begins by introducing the employees
to several people, who share their inspirational
stories. The pursuits, mostly environment and
social in nature, show how ordinary people
can make a profound difference. To get the
employees started on their path, a series of
creative theories and exercises is put into
practice. The inspiration wheel shown here acts
as a random stimulation tool. It uses random
words and images to create free associations,
allowing one to break out of set patterns.

2

1

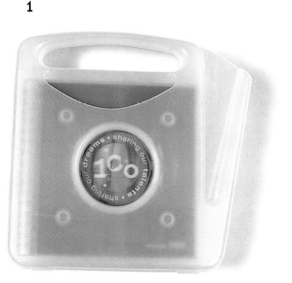

3

CLIENT: DSM N.V.

FIRMS: LAVA GRAPHIC DESIGNERS AND SIGNUM NIEHE EVENTS

CREATIVE DIRECTOR: HANS WOLBERS

DESIGNERS: YKE BARTELS, HEIKE DEHNING, HANS WOLBERS,
AND HUGO ZWOLSMAN

GRAPHIC PRODUCTION: DEF. GRAPHIC PRODUCTIONS

THEORIES: EDWARD DE BONO

PHOTOGRAPHY: MARTIJN BEEKMAN, BILDERBERG FOCUS, BUDI,
ROGER DOHMEN, DRIK, FLIP FRANSSEN, SAKE ELZINGA, FUTURE
FORESTS, GRAMEEN BANK, PETER GRANT, PETER HILZ,
HOLLANDSE HOOGTE, TIMOTHY HURSLEY, PETER HUYS, IMAGE
STORE, JAN JORDAN, CHRIS KEULEN, KONINKLIJK INSTITUUT
VOOR DE TROPEN, RENÉ NUIJENS, MARCUS PETERS, LAURENT
PORDIÉ, STEYE RAVIEZ, SMITHSONIAN INSTITUTE, NIELS
WESTRA, AND HANS WOLBERS

LITHOGRAPHY: PLUSWORKS

PRINTING: DRUKKERIJ KOENDERS & VAN STEIJN

BINDERY: HEPADRU (WIRE-O)

SPECIAL TECHNIQUES: HENK STALLINGA (WATERING CAN DESIGN)

MANUFACTURER: EDIS S.P.A (LENTICULAR STICKER)

Each custom-made silk-screen-printed box contains two small champagne bottles, a clear bag of six chocolates in red foil, a set of sparklers, a capabilities card, and a personalized notecard. Blue crinkle and silver foil add motion and excitement to the already festive package. The fonts used in the promotion, Tanek and Helvetica Condensed, are used on all of BBDI's identity and collateral. Only thirty pieces were made; each was hand-delivered.

With the opening of their affiliate office in Toronto, Bradbury Branding & Design, Inc. (BBDI), was eager to develop their presence and wanted a promotion that would enter this new market with a bang. "For Toronto, we wanted to create something that would serve as a fun and memorable follow-up after an initial presentation," says creative director and designer Catharine Bradbury. "We also wanted something that would be a nice thank-you to our existing clients for their previous business." Thinking about their desire to explode onto the Toronto market, the design firm came up with the idea of using fireworks to convey their message. However, because of the numerous complications associated with shipping explosives, they decided it was best to rework the concept. "Instead, we came up with the idea of using champagne as the big bang," shares Bradbury. "It was a fun item, something that people would certainly hang onto." Considering the events of September 11, just a few months later, the design firm was especially happy they had redirected their focus.

To house their big-bang package, a custom-built box made of ¼-inch (6.35-millimeter) MDF pressed fiberboard was employed. In a bold and dynamic palette of specially mixed colors, each box was silk-screen-printed on all sides, including the bottom. The lid, designed to sit flush on top of the box, has a center hole about ⅝ inch (2 centimeter) in diameter, allowing it to open in a unique way. Inside, a wonderful selection of treats is revealed. "Two bottles of sparkling wine, six chocolates, seven sparklers, and a card explaining the promotion and Bradbury's capabilities were included in each box," details the designer. "In addition, we included a simple notecard, handwritten with a silver pen, to each individual."

Because the bottles already came with a label, the design firm had to soak them in water, remove the existing label, and add a custom-designed silk-screen-printed label. White capsules were applied to the tops of the bottles and, as a finishing touch, a metallic red raffia bow was added. For the chocolates, the design firm approached a local supplier, who custom-wrapped each piece of candy in red foil. The package of six, three milk chocolate and three dark chocolate, were accented with a silver handwritten tag. The sparklers were simply wrapped in a bow. Everything was assembled in-house and hand-delivered to each client.

With a delicious array of sizzle and pop, the big bang promotion shows how BBDI is bursting with the ideas that can ignite any company's business. "All of our promotions have an element of uniqueness, and we always push ourselves to go just a little bit further each time," remarks Bradbury. "This promotion is an investment not only in gaining new clients but also in nurturing our existing client relationships."

TECHNICAL TIPS

When assembling a custom box of this material, carpenter's glue works well. Next, prime the natural brown surface with white latex paint to lessen the absorbency and to give the finishing colors a white surface to reflect off. When you are silkscreen-printing a custom box, you will need to build a jig in order to properly imprint the box on all sides. To remove labels from bottles quickly and easily, soak them in warm water for about an hour. If you plan to use food in your promotion, consider the eating habits of your audience and eliminate potential allergens like nuts. Last, be open to change; allow the piece to evolve. Try not to stay too attached to any one idea, especially if it ultimately does not serve your purpose in the end.

DO IT FOR LESS

Switching from a custom-built box to a cardboard box available in a standard size can save quite a bit of money.

The candy, an assortment of milk and dark chocolates, is wrapped in red foil and packaged in sets of six under the Harden & Huyse label. The hang tags that adorn the chocolates are actually key tags purchased at a local office supply store. The sparkers are wrapped in a raffia bow in sets of seven. Two bottles of champagne, adorned with custom silk-screen-printed labels, are also included in each box.

The capabilities cards are digitally printed on an inkjet printer, mounted on a heavy card stock, and hand-trimmed by the staff. Each notecard is hand-signed using a silver paint pen and fits nicely inside a matching envelope.

FIRM: BRADBURY BRANDING & DESIGN, INC.

CREATIVE DIRECTOR AND DESIGNER: CATHARINE BRADBURY

PRINTING: RSS SIGNS & GRAPHICS (SILK-SCREEN)

MANUFACTURERS: DARYL BASKERVILLE (BOX CREATION AND ASSEMBLY),

AND HARDEN & HUYSE (CHOCOLATES)

2

1

3

What is

☐ rock-n-*roll* ?

☐ *vintage* ?

☐ *feminine* ?

☐ bohemian ?

☐ *ocean* themed ?

☐ ...and has a *seahorse* ?

...ever been faced with a creative challenge that seemed impossible?

We faced just that challenge when fashion designer, Jennifer Nicholson, approached IE Design to create a brand identity for her new vintage couture boutique, *Pearl*. Jennifer, daughter of actor Jack Nicholson, asked for a look that was feminine with a rock-n-roll edge, an ocean theme and bohemian undertones. The boutique would feature two of her own lines. Jennifer Nicholson and Moth, in addition to those of other designers. The Pearl identity had to appropriately convey the high-end image of the store as well as the specific requests of Jennifer. Oh, and by the way, the logo had to include a seahorse and a pearl.

...seemed impossible?

In addition to a huge assortment of printed collateral, we developed gift jewelry pouches, personal hang, fashion hang for hats and shoes, gift boxes, hang tags, and shopping bags.

The success of the Pearl identity system is the "Pearl" Co-partnership between the client and the designer as well as IE Design's open and innovative thinking.

If you would like more information regarding IE Design or more details on the Pearl identity system, please contact:

Ted Cordova
IE Design
Tel: (310) 727-3500
Email: ted@iedesign.net

promotion redefined

Because of the technological advances of the last decade, an overabundance of communications in print, broadcast, and electronic media is being disseminated, and most of it is going by the wayside. Because the effectiveness of the familiar sources of promotion has diminished, creatives are beginning to explore new vehicles and initiatives. They are creating alternative ways for their work to enter and remain viable in the marketplace.

The hard-core sales approach of years past has become passé. To be effective, today's promotion must be engaging and thought-provoking, something that a prospective client will want to retain and utilize. Providing value for the recipient encourages active participation in the overall messaging, greatly increasing the chances for work down the road. "Things that are unabashedly promotional have a shorter life. The recipients will throw away the thing that has expiring value and will keep the thing that speaks to them," adds Sheree Clark of Sayles Graphic Design.

To break through the clutter and make an impact, creatives are finding innovative ways in which to deliver their message. No longer are firms putting out portfolio brochures with self-indulging copy. Promotions are now showing prospective clients what a firm can do in much more innovative ways. "The objects that you send out and give clients should be intelligent, creative, and extraordinary, showing off your firm's personality and thinking," offers Lars Harmsen of MAGMA. "To do that, you have to spend time on your ideas, researching things that are not mainstream." Don Chisholm of dossiercreative agrees. "We have to innovate and create things that did not

exist previously. By breaking the normal paradigms, we can challenge and change perceptions in the way things function, like rethinking the way a brochure works. Because of technology, that is where the industry is going to be pushed."

Designers are pushing themselves to think strategically and to experiment more with unconventional surfaces and printing techniques, interesting bindings and fasteners, and unique constructions and formats. Promotions are also being created as demonstrators, where strategy and creativity come together seamlessly. "The idea of any promotional piece is to go beyond the initial profile enhancement it does for your studio," explains Ric Riordon of the Riordon Design Group, Inc. "Providing examples that are interesting and innovative helps clients make the transition to using you for something similar. It's a springboard for new possibilities." Firms are also hiring consultants and full-time staff from other disciplines to help them conceptualize and think outside the box. "The competition is tough, and everyone is looking to work with the best. At that level, you need to be doing things that are different and stand out," comments Matt Ralph of Plainspoke. "To make a connection, you need to put out a promotion that really has an idea behind it and not just a portfolio of your past work." Creatives who continue to think in narrow terms and rely on the traditional sources for promotion may find themselves limited. Being a little more entrepreneurial in one's approach is key.

Rather than relying on any one venue to deliver their message, firms are thinking in terms of a campaign, penetrating an audience from many fronts. "Whether you are a one-person operation or an agency staffed by 150, an effective and comprehensive marketing and communications program is an absolutely essential business need in order to guarantee the long-term viability and growth of your business. It is the only effective way to target the clients you want, communicate the message you want, shape your market perception—and, ultimately, the direction your business will go in," acknowledges Jonathan Jason of Jason & Jason Visual Communication. "Otherwise, you are essentially assigning the development of your company to good fortune or fate alone."

To supplement their efforts, creatives are investing in public relations and networking opportunities more than ever. Whether a business is relatively new and implementing a pioneering campaign or is a well-established firm in the midst of a relaunch, courting industry trade magazines and book publishers by submitting press releases and feature ideas can attract attention to a particular niche or specialization. "I will contact an editor or writer whose work I admire to let them know that Red Canoe may be up to something of interest," offers cofounder Deb Koch. "I've even put forth a few ideas, offering to write opinion pieces. *HOW* magazine took me up on one idea and gave me the privilege of writing a piece for the 'DeSign Off' column. Everything has the power to lead to something else."

Once a story is picked up by the media, the promotional impact can be extended by announcing the publicity to prospective and existing clients through a newsletter, print or electronic, or an e-mail with a PDF posting. "We have been included in a number of prestigious international design magazines and annuals in the last few years. We have managed to promote our successes by articles and reviews in some of the major national newspapers," shares Nedjeljko Spoljar of Sensus Design Factory. "By increasing general awareness of our studio, this form of promotion has helped a lot in getting higher prices for our work."

Technology has made available new outlets that offer great promotional potential. Interactive Web sites, branded e-mails, online newsletters, and other such venues allow instant and up-to-date information to be cost-effectively delivered to a worldwide audience. "It's a new discipline and an area that is becoming a bigger part of our business," acknowledges Riordon. "Promotions can be custom-tailored with the added benefit of motion and sound, elements that you don't have with a print piece. So what you lose from the tactile side is nicely compensated for by the opportunity to animate and add life to a promotion, making it engaging on a whole different level."

For a more personal approach, event marketing, trade shows, and active involvement in business and professional associations, organizations, and conferences are other ways to connect and build relationships with a targeted audience. "I particularly enjoy trade shows because I can meet potential clients and talk to them about how I can address their communications goals," says Harvey Hirsch of Media Consultants. "Walk through a few trade shows and you will find many companies that are showing their products or services with poorly designed sell sheets, displays, premiums, and so on."

Many creatives are looking within and rethinking their own branding and identity. They are becoming more innovative and strategic—analyzing what they do that is unique and capitalizing on it. An entrepreneurial mindset is in the air, and creatives are just starting to unveil new approaches and possibilities.

repetition of message

A good way to drive home a message is to do it consistently, but with a bit of a twist each time. A pig for Hambly and a sheep for Woolley are repeatedly used in a variety of interesting ways to reinforce the design firm's namesake and ingenuity. "Each year our company sends out a different promotion, and people look forward to what they are going to receive next," adds creative director Bob Hambly. "We always try to create something that is first and foremost fun. It is also important that our promotions have general appeal, are nondenominational, for both sexes, and one-size-fits-all."

Featured here are three promotions from an ongoing series. With a pig embroidered on one and a sheep on the other, a pair of socks promotion travels with its recipient to work and play. It is wrapped in a custom-duplex box with beautifully illustrated winter imagery blind letterpress-printed inside. Baaa-Oink, a kitschy toylike promotion, contains a handmade paddleball with a graphic illustration of a pig on one side and a sheep on the other. The rubber ball attached to the paddle is silkscreen-printed with a pair of nostrils. The whimsical promotion is wrapped in plastic and staple-bound in a fun and entertaining package. The company's mouse pad, again featuring the signature pig and sheep, is sent out at Christmastime with a paper band around the middle that reads, "Not a creature was stirring, not even a mouse." By utilizing an ongoing theme, Hambly and Woolley have successfully built name recognition in the marketplace.

Providing value for the recipient encourages active participation in the overall messaging, greatly increasing the chances for work down the road.

FIRM: HAMBLY & WOOLLEY, INC.

CREATIVE DIRECTORS: BOB HAMBLY
AND BARB WOOLLEY

DESIGNERS: DOMINIC AYRE (MOUSE PAD),
BARB WOOLLEY (PADDLE), AND CHARLIE KIM (SOCKS)

ILLUSTRATION: BOB HAMBLY (PADDLE)
AND ALISON LANG (SOCKS)

PHOTOGRAPHY: CSA ARCHIVES (MOUSE PAD)

PRINTING: RP GRAPHICS (MOUSE PAD),
ANSTEY BOOKBINDING, INC. (PADDLE PACKAGING),
AND LUNAR CAUSTIC PRESS (SOCKS PACKAGING)

MANUFACTURER: RP GRAPHICS (MOUSE PAD)

For a more personal approach, event marketing, trade shows, and active involvement in business and professional associations, organizations, and conferences are other ways to connect and build relationships with a targeted audience.

rounding up the flock

Sayles Graphic Design understands the effectiveness of networking. For the last five years, the firm has organized an event called Birds of a Feather. This annual gathering provides a way for the design firm to intermingle with existing and prospective clientele in a fun and relaxed atmosphere. In the spirit of collaboration, no guest is left unattended and partnership opportunities are encouraged. Photos are taken to document the event, making sure everyone is accounted for. The prints are later sent to each attendee along with the guest list to encourage further contact. After each event, invitees walk away with a special gift and, of course, a business card.

To uniquely kick off each Birds of a Feather function, an intriguing invitation is sent. A three-dimensional, self-mailing piece, decorated with the event's logo and signature graphics, always presents a unique surprise inside. For the theme entitled There's No Stopping Birds of a Feather, a wine cork was enclosed. The ceramic top is decorated with a clear decal printed and sealed with a ceramic glaze. To supplement the event's efforts and keep contacts active year-round, the firm's newsletter is cleverly entitled *Bird Poop*.

To bring in new marketing professionals, Sayles Graphic Design recently adopted a bring-a-guest program. This ingenious idea has significantly increased the number of prospective clients. "I've been able to work on many great design projects, build strong business relationships, and develop some lasting friendships as a result," says principal Sheree Clark.

FIRM: SAYLES GRAPHIC DESIGN

CREATIVE DIRECTOR: JOHN SAYLES

DESIGNERS: JOHN SAYLES AND SOM INTHALANGSY

ILLUSTRATION: JOHN SAYLES

PRINTING: ARTCRAFT, INC.

MANUFACTURERS: ELWOOD PACKAGING, INC. (BOXES), AND GLAZED EXPRESSIONS (WINE STOPPERS)

tokens of appreciation

Personal messages and expressions of gratitude can go a long way toward building lasting relationships with clients. Designer and illustrator Mike Quon has been doing just that with his one-of-a-kind handmade tokens of appreciation. "Art directors are bombarded with e-mails and mass mailings, so I am always trying to do something a little bit more individual," he shares. "There are probably over five hundred art directors in the New York City area that have one of my customized pieces posted on their wall. They all love getting them." Such personal touches leave warm and lasting impressions in the minds of clients. "It is investing in yourself over a long campaign," adds Quon. "It's an ongoing light that says you are vital and active and that working with you will be a lot of fun."

Using a corrugated cardboard surface, Quon paints with acrylics to create a customized image. When he is done, the painted image is hand-cut with a razor blade into a unique shape. The artist individually signs each piece with a black marker, then sends them as postcards to thank clients for their business. In addition to the handmade postcards, Quon also creates one-of-a-kind books—personalized collages sealed with Elmer's glue—that he gives to special clients as gifts. Each token of appreciation he sends goes a long way in building strong clients relations for the future.

FIRM: DESIGNATION INC.

CREATIVE DIRECTOR AND DESIGNER:

MIKE QUON

ILLUSTRATION: MIKE QUON

not your average press release

IE Design had just completed an identity assignment for fashion designer Jennifer Nicholson. The problem that the client posed was indeed challenging: something a bit rock-and-roll, bohemian yet vintage, that somehow included a seahorse. The design firm was so proud of their solution that they wanted to share it with the design community. To capture the attention of busy editors, the creative team knew they had to come up with an approach more engaging than a just a typical press release. "We tried to think of what we could do to get the recipient involved in the piece and not to throw it away," says creative director Marcie Carson. Their solution was an interesting three-dimensional media ensemble.

The design team began by adorning the outside package, a standard-size box, with intriguing text and visual accents. By presenting the design challenge posed by the client, the outside of the self-mailing box entices the viewer to open it. The inside not only unveils the firm's ingenious solution but also contains a sampling of the clever promotion. To make it easy for publications to feature their work, a CD-ROM was enclosed with an image of the complete Pearl identity, including stationery, felt jewelry pouches, garment bags, fabric bags for hats and shoes, gift boxes, hang tags, and a shopping bag.

To keep costs down, everything was produced in-house. The text was printed on blue metallic paper and adhered to the box flat with spray mount, except for the areas where the CD-ROM and business card insert, which were carefully masked. Styrofoam, covered with sandpaper to simulate beach sand, was placed on the bottom of the box to cut down on the movement of the elements within the box. The shells and the shimmering tulle netting laid freely in the box beautifully conveyed an ocean ambience for the Pearl identity to rest while the color scheme and patterns helped to make a connection to the whimsical and vintage clothing line. By creating an interesting spin on a press release, IE Design was able to highlight and call attention to their niche.

*Whether a business is relatively new and implementing
a pioneering campaign or is a well-established firm
in the midst of a relaunch, courting industry trade
magazines and book publishers by submitting press
releases and feature ideas can attract attention to a
particular niche or specialization*

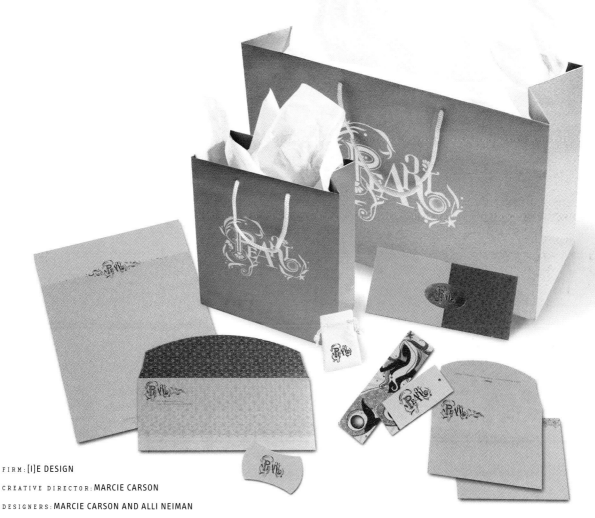

FIRM: [I]E DESIGN

CREATIVE DIRECTOR: MARCIE CARSON

DESIGNERS: MARCIE CARSON AND ALLI NEIMAN

ILLUSTRATION: CYA NELSON

PRINTING: COAST LITHO (PEARL IDENTITY)
AND LASER PRINTER (BOX WRAPPING)

SPECIAL TECHNIQUES: AMEX DIE-CUTTING (PEARL IDENTITY)

MANUFACTURERS: DUMONT PROMOTIONAL IMAGES, INC. (BOXES),
AND LOCAL CRAFT STORE (SHELLS, SANDPAPER, AND FABRIC)

a time for introspection

The dual-functioning package serves as an outer container as well as a desk stand. It is built using a custom duplex of Curious Metallic Ionized and Silktouch Rivercord from Fibermark. The outer surface features the calendar year, a line drawing of the company's building, their logo, and their Web address. Each piece is letterpress-printed with a special mix metallic ink to match the paper, giving it a subtle debossed effect. The iridescent bellyband, which provides assembly instructions, holds the calendar cards in place.

"Every year we try to do a promotion that is a bit of a keeper for our clients," shares art director Ric Riordon. "Given the sensitivity of September 11, we wanted to be a little more thoughtful about what we were communicating as a company—not just to our client base but to the world at large." The idea was to create a promotion that would be a source of inspiration and wisdom in a time where many people were pausing to think and reexamine their lives. With faith and philosophy as driving forces, the design team developed a memorable keepsake calendar. Meant to be a soft sell, the promotion's only point of contact is a Web site listing.

To kick-start the creative process, the design team looked toward the Bible for inspiration, particularly the Old Testament. "We went through a ream of scriptures to determine which were most easily embraced by the largest number of people," recalls Riordon. To ensure the imagery was as thought-provoking as the text, the design team chose a conceptual approach. The images, warm and mostly figurative, work harmoniously with the text to deliver each heartfelt message. Printed in four-color process plus silver, the calendar is calming, reassuring, and stable. An aqueous varnish, applied to both sides of the monthly pages, adds luster, while the rounded edges that appear throughout soften the presentation. A translucent bellyband keeps the cards from moving around within the package and provides a simple diagram to assist in assembly. "The level of excellence in the finishing and details comes together in one package. It is a statement in and of itself," admits creative director Dan Wheaton. "It says what we are capable of and aspire to." Riordon agrees. "We see it as a testimony to our thinking, our craftsmanship, and our creativity."

The biggest challenge was to develop an outer packaging that also served as a stand for the calendar. "Technically, the container was a bit of a twister," admits designer Amy Montgomery. "We wanted a container that was attractive but also functional. A disposable piece would have wasted our efforts." After playing with numerous options, the design team finally came up with the solution they were looking for. Die line in hand, they explored an array of fabrics and papers, producing a few mockups to ensure the proper weight, look, and feel of the piece. To add visual interest, the surface of the custom duplex was letter-press-printed with a special mix metallic. The closure mechanism, made from a purse clasp and a grommet, also serves as a hanging device for the cards. After receiving this promotion, several clients approached the firm about producing a similar project.

TECHNICAL TIPS

When using a custom duplex, always make a mockup before going into production so you can better determine how the materials will look, feel, and assemble. When printing on a colored stock, always run a few tests to make sure the resulting effect is what you want. Don't be afraid to try new materials and explore new ground in your promotions, as they will later serve as a way of exposing clients to other possibilities.

1

The closure mechanism, made from a purse clasp and a grommet, also serves as a hanging device for the calendar. Each month features thought-provoking text accompanied by conceptually driven imagery. The self-contained piece is designed to sit on a desk year-round as a source of strength and hope.

The calendar is displayed in a palette of six subtle tones that repeat to form a visual rhythm. Although they appear to be reproduced as rich duotones, each card is printed in four-color process accented by silver metallic ink. On the reverse side is a double hit of silver. A finishing aqueous varnish is applied to both sides for luster and elegance. The cards are drilled, allowing them to easily hang off the accompanying stand.

3

2

FIRM: THE RIORDON DESIGN GROUP, INC.

CREATIVE DIRECTOR: DAN WHEATON

ART DIRECTOR: RIC RIORDON

DESIGNERS: AMY MONTGOMERY, SHARON PECE, AND SHIRLEY RIORDON

ILLUSTRATION: TIM WARNOCK

PHOTOGRAPHY: RIC RIORDON AND VARIOUS STOCK

PRINTER: CONTACT CREATIVE

BINDERY: CONTACT CREATIVE AND ANSTEY BOOKBINDING

SPECIAL TECHNIQUES: ANSTEY BOOKBINDING

The custom die-cut folder is beautifully printed in three solid PMS colors on Mohawk Navajo 100-lb. cover stock with an overall matte varnish on both sides. A metallic sticker, silk-screen-printed with the company's logo, nicely accents the circular die-cut pattern on the cover. The bilingual package was sent in a silver bag sealed with a consumer product called InstaSealTM/DM.

When Kolégramdesign decided to redirect their company from a production house to a full-service design studio, they knew an image-building brochure was in order. After investigating the competitive landscape, the design firm decided to create a presentation that really stood out strategically as well as creatively. "We picked up profiles of design companies in the region and noticed that they were doing just typical brochures," says creative director and designer Mike Teixeira. "We needed to do something different."

With an artistic flair, the design firm put to work an attractive combination of materials and techniques to deliver their message. The presentation begins with an intricate pocket folder that is embossed, matte varnished, die-cut, and custom scored. A metallic sticker made of brightly brushed stainless polyester adorns the cover with the firm's logo, elegantly silk-screen-printed on top. The promotion's overall theme, Back to the Source, is conveyed through the glossy tint-varnished circular arrows that are framed by the die-cut pattern—handsome but technically challenging to produce—on the front.

Inside the kit, a bilingual introduction card unfolds to reveal a series of six cards. Each card features a softly silhouetted image printed on Mohawk Superfine 100-lb. cover stock, giving it the look and feel of a fine watercolor painting. On the back, eloquently composed text calls attention to key aspects of the firm's unique approach and process. The custom folder closes with an individually numbered business card that inserts into die-cut slots on the back. It is perforated, allowing it to be easily detached and slipped into a business card holder or Rolodex.

To make sure the kit worked the way it should, the design team tested the piece on several people outside their studio to observe different behaviors. They also made several mockups, making sure to analyze every last detail. According to Teixeira, "For the piece to come together, we really had to match up everything, and the die had to be right on." Throughout the entire package, the imagery, text, production techniques, and materials work hand in hand to position Kolégramdesign as a technically innovative design firm with a keen sense for detail. The final design was delivered to prospective clientele in a metallic silver envelope, heat-sealed with a consumer product commonly used for closing food storage bags. The investment the firm made in this brochure has paid off in spades, as business has tripled since its arrival. "It has also set a trend in the region," exclaims Teixeira.

TECHNICAL TIPS

To make sure a complex pocket folder with various folds, scores, and die-cuts works the way it is designed to, test it on people outside of the design community to see how they open and interact with what you have created. Don't be afraid to use ordinary consumer products in order to produce the piece in-house. They are usually a lot cheaper than their industrial counterparts and often work just as well.

The folder, which boasts an array of interesting folds and angles, is embossed and scored with a series of width options for expandability. A business card, conveniently attached to the back of the folder, is individually numbered and perforated for easy detachment.

The six die-cut cards are held together by a gate-folded wrapper that also serves as an introductory device for the package. Each card features a concept image and supportive text in both French and English; these work together to communicate the firm's process and design philosophy. The artistic look and feel appeals to Kolégramdesign's predominately cultural clientele.

1

2

3

FIRM: KOLÉGRAMDESIGN

CREATIVE DIRECTOR AND DESIGNER: MIKE TEIXEIRA

PHOTOGRAPHY: HEADLIGHT INNOVATIVE IMAGERY

PRINTING: IMPRIMERIE DU PROGRÈS (BROCHURE)

AND SÉRIGRAPHIE ALBION (LABEL)

SPECIAL TECHNIQUES: CAPITAL BOX (DIE-CUTTING)

AND STYLEX 3D (EMBOSSING)

MANUFACTURER: ASSOCIATED BAGS CO.

idea
generators

The simple, but elegant, package is made of a custom duplex white corrugated board adhered to a smooth gray text stock. It is sent as a self-mailer with a personalized letter inside.

"Our firm's niche is not a specific style or look but an attitude that is expressed by having ideas and creating unique solutions for our clients," says creative director Oliver A. Krimmel. To communicate their personalized approach, the creative team came up with a simple, yet clever, promotion. "I am always searching for things that relate to our philosophy and that transport our message in an emotional manner," offers Krimmel. "With this promotion, I wanted to focus on the basis behind our work to create in people's minds the thought that our firm is synonymous with good ideas. If good ideas are needed, i_d buero, which means 'idea office,' has them." With that in mind, the biggest challenge was simplifying the message and presenting it in an intriguing way. "Reducing is always the most difficult task," explains Krimmel. "You do not want to leave important things out, but you also don't want to add one more thing too many."

With sketching and journal writing as the primary ways in which good ideas commence, the design team chose paper and pencil as the perfect vehicles to instill their message. They looked at various materials and containers, from blister packs to sewn packages, to house the idea-generating duo. "Finally we came up with the idea of using a notebook, where the pencil is wrapped by an elegant, but not overdone, cardboard box," shares Krimmel. To work out the details of the outer structure, the creative team referred to packaging design books, researching folding methods and boxes of many shapes and sizes.

The resulting format boasts a long and slender custom duplex box made from a thin microcardboard that was laminated to gray stock. Its extended flaps unfold to reveal a perfect-bound notebook with silver cut edges. "It's an old manner of putting beaten metal together with egg white on plain abraded book sides. But nowadays, you can only afford the industrial way. With a heat of about 120°C, the metal leaves are activated and pressed onto the paper," explains Krimmel. "The process can be done in a range of metallic colors." Inside the notebook, a silver hot foil–embossed white pencil with the words *gute Idee*, which means "good idea," and *schlechte Idee*, which means "bad idea," can be found. "There is a very tiny blur between common materials and techniques and modified details, which garner high attention," notes Krimmel. "The differences are most important." The copy, the format, and the special production accents work together to communicate the company's message. The only point of contact is a Web address. The piece was sent as a self-mailer along with a personalized letter to a targeted group of clientele.

TECHNICAL TIPS

The silver can be applied to the surface only after the pages are cut and bound. Special attention needs to be given to the bindery process, which must be precise in order for the silver to adhere correctly. Custom duplex stocks do not always work the way you would like them to. Always produce an exact mock-up and analyze every last detail before you go into full production.

Inside is a perfect-bound notebook lined with silver trim, a fused metal technique normally used on Bibles. Nestled inside the die-cut pages is a white hot foil–embossed pencil. The only point of contact in the promotion is the company's Web address, which is centered on the pencil.

On the lead side of the pencil, the words *gute Idee*, which means "good idea," are imprinted, while on the rubber eraser side of the pencil *schlechte Idee*, which means "bad idea," is imprinted. The simple design and strong messaging shows how sometimes less is more.

1

2

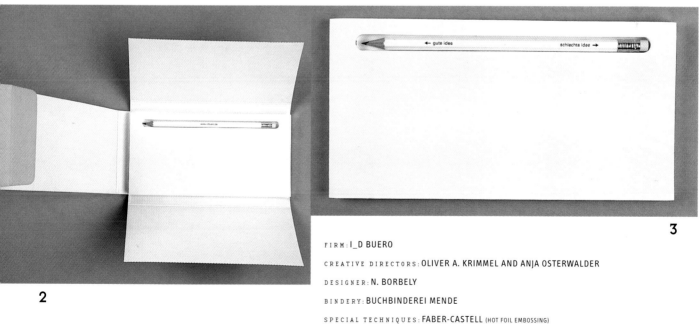

3

FIRM: I_D BUERO

CREATIVE DIRECTORS: OLIVER A. KRIMMEL AND ANJA OSTERWALDER

DESIGNER: N. BORBELY

BINDERY: BUCHBINDEREI MENDE

SPECIAL TECHNIQUES: FABER-CASTELL (HOT FOIL EMBOSSING)

MANUFACTURERS: BUCHBINDEREI MENDE AND FABER-CASTELL

moving
announcement

Douglas Joseph Partners had moved just a hop, skip, and a jump down the road from 11999 San Vicente Boulevard to 11812 San Vicente Boulevard and needed to let people know about it. "Our goal was to announce our move and to do it in such a way that it was memorable," recalls creative director and president Doug Joseph. Because the piece was a moving announcement, a flipbook format seemed the perfect way to convey the information.

The game plan was to animate a man walking across the page, starting at the old address and moving toward the new location—simple, right? Well, not exactly. The feat required the designer not only to plot various gestures that simulated the movements of a man walking but also to create a character interesting enough to look at. In addition, the figure had to remain consistent in shape and height throughout in order to make the animation believable and seamless. The designer had to do all this within a given size and number of pages that were predetermined based on maximizing the press sheet. To get the mechanics just right, several dummies were produced.

The next task was to identify the paper and bindery that would best carry the subtle message. Providing just the right opacity and ease of use, Fraser Papers Pegasus 100-lb. smooth text in brilliant white was found to be the best stock for the job. Double bronze rivets were the clear bindery winner. "For a book whose sole purpose is to be flipped through over and over again, perfect binding would have failed eventually," adds Joseph. "The rivets will never fail." The entire piece was printed on one side only in a palette indicative of the firm's new office space.

To ship the animated announcement, a custom die-cut fluted cardboard box was created. It was designed to protect the flipbook, make it stand out in the mail, and be cost-effective. The mailing labels that seal the outer package were also created specifically for the moving announcement. The simple and straightforward piece was sent to existing and prospective clients as well as vendors. "Most people kept the flipbook on their desks because it was fun to pick up every now and then," shares Joseph. "We knew we were successful based on the number of calls and comments we received afterwards. In past moves, we've done simple announcement cards and never heard a word from anybody."

TECHNICAL TIPS

The animation has to be just right for a flipbook to work. Make several dummies, checking the fluidity of movement and the overall graphic appeal. Before the book is bound, make a final dummy from the press sheets as a last-minute check. To save money, maximize your press sheet.

By using a flipbook, Douglas Joseph Partners made memorable their relocation from 11999 San Vicente Boulevard to 11812 San Vicente Boulevard. The color palette throughout, PMS 617, PMS 7531, and a custom-matched yellow-green, are all taken from the new office space.

The animated moving announcement is sent to clients and vendors in a custom die-cut package made of fluted cardboard, both attractive and functional. It is sealed with a label designed especially for the announcement.

1

2

FIRM: DOUGLAS JOSEPH PARTNERS

CREATIVE DIRECTORS: DOUG JOSEPH AND SCOTT LAMBERT

DESIGNER: MARK SCHWARTZ

ILLUSTRATION: MARK SCHWARTZ

PRINTING: ANDERSON LITHOGRAPH

BINDERY: JENCO

A miniportfolio, housed in a translucent, orange, plastic box, is the device used to introduce Platform Creative to prospective clients. The portfolio pages, printed internally using a Xerox 7700DN dual-sided color printer, highlight the quality and diversity of the firm's work. The package is labeled front and back, shrink-wrapped, and sent as a self-mailer.

Sometimes a single mailing is just not enough. Clients often must be reminded several times before a message yields a response. To pack a one-two punch, Platform Creative developed a series of mailings to introduce themselves and their work to prospective clients. The first mailing, a miniportfolio of sorts, helped establish credibility and show off Platform's breath and experience in the marketplace. "The goal was to legitimize our services with our previous successes," says creative director and designer Robert Dietz. "In most cases, designers send out promotions to get a portfolio review which will then lead to a relationship. Our thought was to get the portfolio review out of the way right up front." The firm could tailor the customizable piece to any prospective client's needs. "We can also take feedback from pervious recipients and refine the type of information included for future mailings," adds Dietz.

To house and accent their work, the design team explored an array of materials before they decided on a brilliant orange plastic. "The impact is immediate," shares Dietz. "The translucent plastic acts as a tease in that you can see something bright and substantial inside. The color demands notice when combined with other mail and materials on someone's desk." The plastic, chosen for its visual impact and relationship to the company's branded color scheme, was purchased in large sheets and trimmed to create miniboxes, wire-o bound covers, and presentation portfolios. Because of the plastic's translucency, type can be clearly read from the printed material underneath, eliminating the need to imprint the plastic itself. The biggest challenge was nailing down the mechanics of the box; numerous changes were made before a design with just the right look, strength, and locking mechanism was established. The completed package was labeled and shrink-wrapped to minimize damage in delivery.

The follow-up promotion was designed to mimic the look and feel of the first mailing yet still have its own identity. Thus, the second mailing was delivered in bright orange, translucent envelopes. "The goal of the cards was to expound our business philosophies and reinforce key attributes of how we think and solve problems," offers Dietz. "We wanted the cards to map back to the idea that strong messaging, marketing, and visual platforms are the basics for a successful brand." The cards, designed to be interactive, play on the firm's name and philosophy. Each card has a key word on one side and a business statement on the back. A bellyband, used to keep the message-driven cards in their proper order, provides simple instructions on how they can be used to build a structure or platform. As a continuation of the overall messaging, more cards can be created and sent to the same target audience at a later date.

TECHNICAL TIPS

Work closely with your vendors, utilizing them for technical assistance when determining mechanical feasibility. Whenever you use a new material, create prototypes and perform test mailings to make sure the chosen vehicle successfully delivers your message intact. When using plastics, budget time for adjustments and revisions before final manufacturing. Don't hesitate to solicit feedback from existing clients about your promotions. Their insight can be quite valuable.

2

3

The set of die-cut cards, printed on 100-lb Topcoat cover gloss on two sides, is held in place by a bellyband. The orange, translucent envelope looks and feels like the first mailing. The address label, symbolic of a three-dimensional box or platform, is consistent with the firm's letterhead, business cards, envelopes, and Web site. The stackable cards provide interaction and make a connection to the firm's philosophy that strong messaging and visual platforms are the basics for a successful brand.

An 11- by 17-inch (28- by 43-centimeter) portfolio, used as a presentation device at meetings, utilizes the same translucent plastic to make a connection to the promotional campaign.

1

FIRM: PLATFORM CREATIVE GROUP, INC.
CREATIVE DIRECTOR: ROBERT DIETZ
DESIGNERS: ROBERT DIETZ, KATHY THOMPSON, AND JIN KWON
ILLUSTRATION: JIN KWON AND KATHY THOMPSON
PHOTOGRAPHY: IRIDIO (PORTFOLIOS) AND PHOTODISC (CARDS)
PRINTING AND BINDERY: GAC ALLIED
MANUFACTURERS: ACTION ENVELOPE AND GENERAL BINDERY COMPANY

3

2

the
sequel

Several years ago, Modern Dog Communications embarked on their first deck-of-cards promotion. It featured fifty-two of the firm's best poster designs and was a huge success, as it brought in long-term business and sold in several museums. "With our first deck, my business partner was lecturing in Salt Lake City and people came up and bought the cards. One guy, who was a student at the time, still had our cards and e-mailed us," shares creative director and designer Robynne Raye. "He is now working in Japan for one of the largest retail clothing companies. For the past two and a half years, he has been our biggest client." When a promotion is a functional object that a prospective client wants to retain and utilize, the chance for work down the road increases greatly. "I always try to design things that will not get thrown away. I hate promotions that are unusable and forgettable," remarks Raye. "Promotions should outlive their intended use or else they become landfill. Because our cards are usable, we get repeated exposure from them."

Once the first set of cards depleted, the firm thought it was time for a sequel. Again they looked to their vast collection of poster work for visual support. The second deck features a new series of projects in the highly graphic look for which Modern Dog is known. The cards sit nicely in a custom-designed box. The hand-painted look of the cover illustration and the graphic use of type play off the signature-style posters that are uniformly displayed inside. Because the promotion was expensive to produce, the design firm chose to cut costs by collating the deck in-house. "All of the cards were printed on one sheet, but when they were delivered, they came in different boxes," comments Raye. "We had to set up a space just for putting the decks together." To keep the task organized and to save as much time as possible, a jig was built as a convenient way to sort each deck, alleviating the cumbersome process of going from box to box.

Entitled Peep, this lively and entertaining deck of oversized playing cards packs both a promotional and a merchandising punch. "The series acts like a mini-portfolio. It's a great leave-behind when we meet someone for the first time," says Raye. "We also sell them through our Web site." Only 3,500 were produced. "For us, it has opened a lot of doors and gotten us into places to which, normally, graphic designers would not even go, like museums. This type of promotion has come back years later and has definitely paid for itself."

TECHNICAL TIPS

If you decide to collate a deck of cards in-house, you should set up a system to keep the job organized. Try to find outlets in which to sell the playing cards to help cover the heavy production expenses.

DO IT FOR LESS

Producing an oversize custom deck of cards is expensive. To cut costs significantly, stick to a standard-size deck and locate a vendor who has a die already made. Hand-collating the deck in-house is time-consuming but a definite must if you are budget conscious.

The set of commercial art playing cards is the second in a series for the Seattle-based firm. The oversized deck, with its bright palette, is meant to be fun and engaging. The cards fit nicely inside a custom-designed box that is coated with varnish.

The deck of cards features the poster work of Modern Dog Communications. Each featured project is supplemented by a brief description, revealing the client, title, completion date, print size, and method of reproduction. The cards are printed in four colors on Utopia Premium 150-lb. cover stock; an overall aqueous varnish provides protection and durability.

FIRM: MODERN DOG COMMUNICATIONS, INC.

CREATIVE DIRECTORS: MICHAEL STRASSBURGER
    AND ROBYNNE RAYE

DESIGNER: ROBYNNE RAYE

ILLUSTRATION: ROBYNNE RAYE

PRINTING: COLORGRAPHICS

2

1

flickering of light

The promotion is revealed behind a translucent vellum wrap that offers instructions in assembling the tea light shade. A small white candle accompanies the promotion.

Heads, Inc., wanted to put together a warm and inviting holiday greeting to give to clients, colleagues, and friends. Inspired by the transcendent quality of a flickering flame, creative director and designer So Takahashi decided to develop an intricate shade to capture candlelight's intrinsic beauty. "I liked the challenge of making something even more special through my design," he adds.

Because the company specializes in three-dimensional design—packaging, product design, and window displays—it was important that the promotion encompass aspects of this niche. "Three-dimensional design is my counterattack on computer-based two-dimensional design, which is an intangible practice," acknowledges Takahashi. "I am always trying to apply my ideas in different media because I don't believe in borders in the design field."

After looking at several approaches, the designer chose thin aircraft-grade birch plywood as his working surface and laser cutting as the vehicle to deliver his message. "I explored many three-dimensional designs, using different materials and techniques," he details. "I like the wood surface because it is earthy and far from synthetic, and it gives off a natural wooded scent once the candle is lit. Since I live and work in Manhattan, a big manmade artificial city, the usage of natural elements is very attractive." The wood was purchased in 12- by 24-inch (30- by 61-centimeter) sheets, making roughly five to six shades per sheet. The biggest challenge came from the fragility of the wooden surface. The wood had to be thin to allow it to bend 360 degrees but, at the same time, it had to be durable enough to withstand the laser-cutting process.

For a holiday season touch, the designer created a snowflake pattern that not only looked graphically interesting but also allowed light to pass through in an even and luminous way. "For the layout and type, I wanted to make something that created a nice effect when the candlelight shone through it," shares Takahashi. "The geometric pattern casts beautiful circular shadows that appeal to me." Text was also added along the bottom to complete the message. The self-assembling piece was sent flat, along with a candle. Instructions on how to put together the tea light shade were economically imprinted by a laser printer on a translucent vellum paper.

TECHNICAL TIPS

If you want to cut into a thin wood surface, use a laser process rather than a die. Traditional die-cutting leads to technical difficulties in producing fine details against the grain of the wood. When you are trying to innovate, it is important to experiment and play, exploring disciplines outside of graphic design. Too often, we are so afraid to fail that we don't venture outside our safety zone. By taking risks, we open doors to new possibilities.

The tea light shade is made of aircraft-grade birch plywood. Laser cutting is used to establish the shape and imprint the surface with a snowflake pattern and holiday greeting.

When the candle is lit within the shade, a nice warm glow of light flickers through the intricate design.

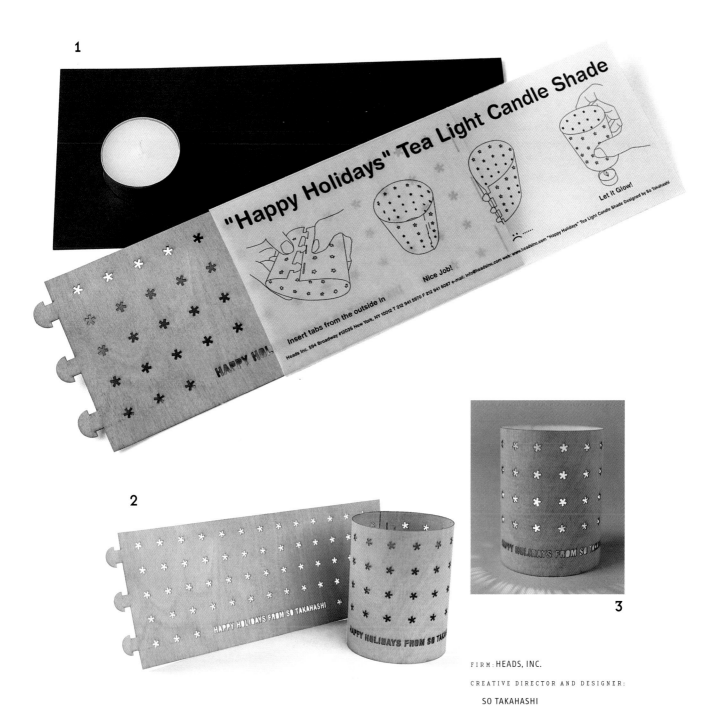

1

2

3

FIRM: HEADS, INC.

CREATIVE DIRECTOR AND DESIGNER:
SO TAKAHASHI

SPECIAL TECHNIQUES: ELASERWORKS

MANUFACTURER: LOCAL STORE (WOOD AND CANDLE)

structural
innovation

Weidlinger Associates, Inc., was celebrating their fiftieth anniversary and wanted to share it with long-term clients and prospects. Known worldwide for their structural engineering creativity, the firm sought to do something memorable and lasting. The creative team at Nassar Design was brought in to assist. Working collaboratively, they discussed the company's diverse range of work, core values, overall branding, and positioning in the marketplace. After an intensive brainstorming session, the design team proposed an interesting idea: to announce the anniversary year with a structural competition meant to engage clients to actively participate in the celebration. The marketing department at Weidlinger bought into the concept wholeheartedly.

To capture the attention of the structural engineering firm's busy target market, the invitation had to go beyond the norm. With that in mind, the designers went to work developing a creative and unique approach. The result was a custom die-cut, three-dimensional poster that featured Weidlinger Associates' latest achievements in an exciting and innovative way. "The 16- by 16-inch (41- by 41-centimeter) animated poster was a portfolio survey of the transportation and architectural engineering divisions of the firm," says Weidlinger's communications director, Helen Goddard. "It emphasized the skeletal abstract beauty of the projects we have designed." The interactive piece encouraged recipients to submit a unique structure. To assist in the design, an origami expert was called in. "We relied partly on the expertise of a specialist to determine the number of panels needed to help our receivers in creating, folding, and scoring an origami piece," creative director and designer Nelida Nassar adds. "We started by identifying the basic geometric forms, and, bit by bit, we retained the square format as the most responsive to our needs; it could fold and unfold without being cumbersome."

The anniversary poster was packaged inside a custom die-cut cardboard box along with the competition rules and an invitation to the celebration. The best entries were compiled in a black-and-white brochure, the purpose of which "was to visually record the winning entries and to document the success and enthusiasm the competition generated," notes Nassar. Both the party and the competition were a huge success. Over five hundred people participated, and the winning structures, based on innovative excellence, structural elegance, and economy of means, were featured in the company's Web site, newsletter, and in the print media. Many of the structural creations are still on permanent display at Weidlinger Associates.

TECHNICAL TIPS

For an origami project to work, it is important that a quality die be made to ensure proper folding and registration accuracy. The choice of paper is also crucial. Selecting a stock that is either too thick or too thin may result in unwanted tearing and ripping at the perforations. When custom-designing a box, always make a mockup first to ensure the necessary materials fit inside just right. Consulting a specialist—in this case, an origami expert—is a good idea, as he or she can assist in designing a structural base conducive to the creation of other structures.

The three-dimensional invitation, housed in a custom die-cut box, is both dynamic and engaging. The unique scores, cuts, and folds encourage recipients to create their own unique structures. Also included in the waffle-sealed package are the rules of the competition and an invitation to attend the celebration. The corporate color, PMS 307, is used throughout on Mohawk Superfine 130-lb. Navajo double-thick brilliant white paper. An overall aqueous matte varnish is applied for durability.

Shown are just some of the structures created in the Wai-o-gami competition.

2

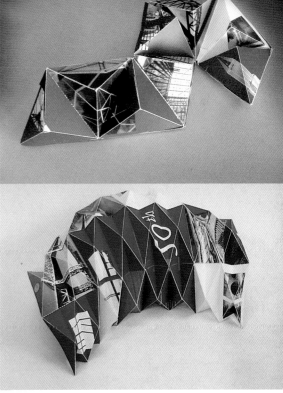

1

CLIENT: WEIDLINGER ASSOCIATES, INC.

FIRM: NASSAR DESIGN

CREATIVE DIRECTOR: NELIDA NASSAR

DESIGNERS: NELIDA NASSAR AND MARGARITA ENCOMIENDA

PHOTOGRAPHY: WEIDLINGER ARCHIVES

PRINTING AND BINDERY: MERRILL/DANIELS

SPECIAL TECHNIQUES: DIE TECH ASSOCIATES (DIE) AND PETER ENGEL (ORIGAMI ADVISER)

MANUFACTURER: ROMANOW CONTAINER

sight and sound

Gerald & Cullen Rapp, Inc., needed an elaborate, high-impact advertising piece to showcase their team of anaglyph, pop-up, and sound technology producers. They also wanted "to promote the illustrator, who did the background, as well as the design firm and printer I was representing at the time," adds creative director and agent Gerald Rapp. Working collaboratively, the team of experts developed a large-format, three-panel, letter-folded technology extravaganza.

For an element of surprise, the cover was designed as a standard black-and-white, two-dimensional brochure with the tagline "Say Goodbye to Flat Advertising." Once inside, a highly saturated color presentation complete with pop-ups, sound, and anaglyphic imagery unfolded. "Our brains are wired to expect something two-dimensional, especially when it arrives flat in the mail," comments paper engineer Phillip Fickling. "A pop-up adds huge emotional impact to your message, thereby increasing its retention. Pop-ups just have that wow factor." Throughout the excitement-filled promotion, each custom-designed pop-up was directly adhered to the surface with tabs. The overall use of paper pop-ups adds physical depth to the otherwise two-dimensional piece.

The recording that accents the technology-based piece utilized a small, battery-operated sound chip to carry its message. The inner workings were physically shown to demonstrate how the technology operates. In most cases, the sound chip is hidden within the constructs of a piece. "There are chips that will record almost any message, and they are typically used in small runs to a narrowly targeted audience," details Rapp. "If you are doing a larger quantity, you can use a prerecorded standard message that is already built into the chip." For this technology, there is a wide array of existing sounds at varying time intervals available.

The most intriguing aspect of the piece was its use of anaglyph technology. The 3-D glasses and stereoscopic viewers beckon the viewer to actively participate. "If someone receives a piece of direct mail or opens a magazine and sees a pair of 3-D glasses, there is something terrifically compelling about it," shares anaglyphic consultant Steve Aubrey. "The notice factor and the ability to rise above the general noise level are probably the greatest advantages of the medium in the competitive marketplace." With the use of anaglyph imagery, the subject matter is transformed from a flat reproduction to a spatially engaging and highly dimensional experience.

Acting as a demonstrative device, the high-impact, eye-catching brochure showed prospective clients the potential that dimension and sound could bring to their advertising. The effect is similar to when, in the *Wizard of Oz*, Dorothy breaks free from the confines of Kansas and enters into a magical, new world. As stated in the brochure, "Readers will experience your advertising in an entirely new way when they leave the overcrowded land of flat advertising and step into the new world of state-of-the-art printacular magic."

TECHNICAL TIPS

If you are interested in using anaglyphic, sound chip, or pop-up technologies, it is highly advisable to bring in experts to work with you as early as the concept stage. Engaging a good technical consultant allows you to effectively utilize each medium to its fullest. The Graphic Arts Technical Foundation (GATF) is a good place to start your search for specialists in anaglyphic technology.

When using pop-ups, produce an accurate mockup to ensure the art is where you want it to be and the paper is the right weight for the job. Also, pay attention to the paper's grain direction. As a general rule, creases should run parallel to the grain. To address durability concerns, remember that creases last longer than perforations and, over time, mechanical joins last longer than adhesives.

For anaglyphic usage, avoid using colors that approach saturated red and cyan, the two separation filters commonly used in 3-D eyewear. The closer you get to these colors the more your image will seem ultraneon and unnatural. However, if that is the effect you are looking for, you can exploit these colors by introducing them into the scene as accents.

There are two ways in which to show something in 3-D. One is by printing the left- and the right-eye images on top of each other using complementary colors. When you put on the red and cyan filtered glasses, you get the illusion of depth. Another way is by using stereo viewers, where the two images are physically segregated and do not require color separation filters. The advantage to this process is that it imposes no color limitations. The down side is that it is a bit more expensive per unit to produce.

1

The piece presents itself like a traditional two-dimensional brochure, creating an element of surprise once opened. It is sent in a custom-designed envelope with a cover letter to agency account executives, creative directors, and corporate communications people.

2

Inside the high-impact promotional brochure, three technologies—anaglyphic, sound chip recording, and pop-ups—are demonstrated. The piece is four-color offset-printed and laminated for durability.

DO IT FOR LESS

When using pop-ups, design your piece to minimize handwork, saving valuable time. It is also a good idea to stick to traditional paper, as more elaborate materials, like acetate windows and synthetics, increase the cost significantly.

If you know you want to employ anaglyphs in your promotion, remember that it is most cost-effective to photograph the piece in 3-D. If you are using illustration, a 3-D computer-generated image will also save in 2-D-to-3-D conversion time and money. Many 3-D software programs have stereo converters built in, making the process user-friendly.

1

FIRM: GERALD & CULLEN RAPP, INC.

CREATIVE DIRECTOR: GERALD RAPP

DESIGNER: BLUE BRICK DESIGN

ILLUSTRATION: SHARMEN LIAO

PHOTOGRAPHY: STEVE SPELMAN
 AND KENNETH WILLARDT

PRINTING: FOX PRESS, INC.

SPECIAL TECHNIQUES: USA PRINT & POPS
 AND ANAGLYPHIC IMAGING

2

WE'VE MOVED

MANAGEMENT
LEVY CREATIVE

300 E. 46th Street
Suite 8E
NYC 10017
TEL (212) 687-6463
FAX (212) 661-4839
www.levycreative.com

WE'VE MOVED

MANAGEMENT
CREATIVE

300 E. 46th Street
Suite 8E
NYC 10017
TEL (212) 687-6463
FAX (212) 661-4839
www.levycreative.com

WE'VE MOVED

MANAGEMENT
CREATIVE

WE'VE MOVED

MANAGEMENT
LEVY CREATIVE

300 E. 46th Street
Suite 8E
NYC 10017
TEL (212) 687-6463
FAX (212) 661-4839
www.levycreative.com

300 E. 46th Street
Suite 8E
NYC 10017
TEL (212) 687-6463
FAX (212) 661-4839
www.levycreative.com

the art of direct mail

In today's demanding marketplace, direct mail promotions need to be innovative from both a strategic and creative standpoint to leave a lasting impression on prospective buyers. They must instantly grab the recipients' attention, motivating them to look inside and participate in the overall messaging. A good direct mail promotion encourages interaction. To achieve this, firms are no longer doing mass mailings; instead, they are spending their time and money producing well-targeted promotions that speak to the audience in a very thought-provoking and personal way. "Your potential client comes across so many direct mail pieces all day long. You want to create something that your audience will want to hold onto and not something that ends up in the wastebasket," notes Charlotte Noruzi of Question Design. "The more personal and functional a promo is, the better." Harvey Hirsch of Media Consultants agrees. "Put yourself into the mind of the receiver and try to develop something that makes you smile, laugh, or gets you emotionally involved." The best promotions create an experience for the recipient.

To create distinction, mailers are increasingly incorporating alternative materials, formats, and techniques. The use of scented papers, three-dimensional packaging, add-ons, and textural accents all help engage the audience by appealing to the senses. "To make sure we are creating innovative and inspirational solutions, I try to keep everyone here refreshed and aware of what is going on in printing, production, and paper. I really utilize my vendor resources," offers Marcie Carson of IE Design. "Any time our printing reps get something

interesting in their shops or the paper manufacturers start a new line, they always call on us and let us know about them." Noruzi adds, "It is important to keep on top of the latest trends, equipment, mediums, and materials to come up with a different way to do something. Always innovate, experiment, doing whatever it takes to stand apart." The architecture of the, once typical brochure is evolving.

Copywriting, which once played second fiddle to design, has become an integral and vital part of the creative process. Most firms now see it as the foundation from which a promotion is built—and rightly so. Direct mail copy, a one-on-one form of communication, is strongest when targeted and motivational in nature. "We believe copy should always be crisp and succinct, because people don't want to have to read a lot of it. You must quickly address the recipient's needs, wants, and aspirations, and why they should consider your product or service," reminds David Collins of Grafik. "Whether the tone of the copy is light or somber, it must provide the information in a way that readers can appreciate and understand. In other words, it's not about you, it's about them." The whole package has to come together in a manner consistent with the overall concept, and every part of the promotion has to work hard doing its job: supporting and delivering a company's message. Strategies vary from single hits to a

series of mailings that function like a campaign. Direct mail is also being integrated with other promotional vehicles.

In a marketplace that speaks to reduced budgets and limited resources, creatives are doing all they can to make sure their promotions are as effective as they can be before they are delivered. A lot more time is spent doing mockups and analyzing just how recipients will read and use what is produced. Test mailings are conducted to ensure promotions arrive the way they should; deviations are corrected immediately. List maintenance is also important, and updates are made annually. Companies are developing coded systems to track their promotions, and follow-up procedures are becoming a permanent part of the overall process. "In today's competitive marketplace, it is critical that an aggressive program of telemarketing be employed if you want results," advises Hirsch. "I never wait for a prospect to get back to me." Business reply cards, toll-free numbers, telemarketing, and other such methods are all being explored.

Direct mail, one of the most responsive and effective forms of advertising, allows a message to be disseminated to a targeted audience in a personal and customized fashion. Because of technology, databases can be manipulated into solid mailing lists, which can target any market with pinpoint accuracy. With a captivating and engaging design, an accurate and well-targeted mailing list, and an incentive to respond, direct mail is a great way to go after new prospects as well as generate repeat business.

FIRM: QUESTION DESIGN

CREATIVE DIRECTOR AND DESIGNER: CHARLOTTE NORUZI

ILLUSTRATION: CHARLOTTE NORUZI

PRINTING: EPSON PRINTER (MASK)

MANUFACTURER: KATE'S PAPERIE (RIBBON)

seasonal message

"Each promotion is a chance to explore a new medium and a new way of doing something," offers designer and illustrator Charlotte Noruzi. "It is important to be as innovative as you can, making your piece memorable and personal. The more it feels like your audience is receiving a gift, the better." By using an unconventional vehicle—a handmade mask—the multi-faceted artist was able to attract the attention of her publishing audience. The copy, reading "Kiss Someone this Halloween," helped tie in the season and, at the same time, highlight the artist's recently illustrated cover for a book entitled *Kissing Kate*. "The other intent of the promo was to actually have my audience wear the mask to a Halloween party and create a buzz," shares Noruzi.

The stylistically hand-painted mask was reproduced on heavyweight matte paper using an Epson printer. Each piece was hand-cut and assembled by the artist. A shimmering ribbon adorned the playful promotion, allowing it to be tied on or hung if so desired. The highly illustrative promotion was sent in a hand-lettered vellum envelope. The brilliant yellow color of the translucent outer package nicely complemented the whimsical purple mask inside. "I wanted my audience to be able to see through the envelope for their curiosity to be aroused as to what was inside," Noruzi adds. A limited run was created and mailed during October. "Targeting a small but specific audience is a much more successful and productive path," claims the artist. "It's better to know twenty-five prospective clients personally than one thousand impersonally or not at all." Targeted toward art directors and editors at publishing houses, the Halloween mask promotion was Noruzi's way of calling attention to her ingenuity, creativity, and vast array of skills. "I think uniqueness is important," she concludes. "In this age of computerization, a handmade promotion is a breath of fresh air."

FIRM: MEDIA CONSULTANTS

CREATIVE DIRECTOR AND DESIGNER:
HARVEY HIRSCH

ILLUSTRATION: ERIC ROSE

PRINTING: SHARP AR-C250 DIGITAL COLOR COPIER

SPECIAL TECHNIQUES: STEEL RULE DIES (FISH DIE)
AND HOLOGRAPHIC FINISHING (PRESSING)

making it pop

"I have been folding paper since I was a kid, and the finished piece always elicited a great response when I handed it to someone," recalls creative director and designer Harvey Hirsch. "When I started my own marketing graphics firm, I printed an illustrated fish on my black-and-white copier. It was a smiling fish that said 'Thanks for Swimming with Us.' I sent them to our clients, and the response was so positive that I had some printed in four color." After an assignment from Sharp Electronics to produce a dealer-directed campaign launching the company's digital color copier and printer, Hirsch made a breakthrough discovery. With this new technology he could decorate, personalize, and make dimensional his origami fish mailers with the press of a button.

Printed on a Sharp AR-C250 digital color copier using a metallic paper, each origami fish mailer can be adorned with any typeface and color, allowing modifications on the fly. The fish and custom envelope are scored and nicked to facilitate folding and removal.

To create distinction, promotions are incorporating alternative materials, formats, and techniques. The use of scented papers, three-dimensional packaging, add-ons, and textural accents all help engage the audience by appealing to the senses.

For alignment purposes, each sheet of paper has a hole that acts like a registration mark. "Adjusting the artwork on the computer so it fits precisely over the pattern when it prints requires only a few clicks and a few test sheets," notes Hirsch. Each fish is adhered to the promotional card with Velcro, making it removable.

The eye-catching, three-dimensional mailer was so successful that it opened new opportunities for the marketing and creative firm to explore. "I can now license my products and technology to selected clients by SIC and Zip codes," shares Hirsch. "This enabled me to spin off a whole new corporation, called Pop'N'Fold Papers, Inc., with a product line so innovative that I can offer almost thirty three-dimensional products that can all be personalized in short runs. This gives a user the opportunity to mail a high-response mailer and test offers, copy, prices, pitches, etc., without a plate change, and it can be in the mail in hours, not weeks. These little fish helped me build a business."

kinetic announcement

When it came time to relocate their offices, Levy Creative Management knew they had to send out an announcement that was far from ordinary. Working collaboratively with designer Mirko Ilić, they came up with an interesting and cost-effective solution: a moving announcement that moves! Each mailer, printed in fluorescent inks on Gilbert Gilclear 28-lb. vellum, was die-cut to reveal the firm's logo. The die-cut shape, printed with the new contact information, was put to work, moving around loosely within a clear plastic envelope. "As it travels through the mail, the Ls move and, no matter where the shapes fall, you can always read at least one or two words," explains Ilić. "The L also becomes almost like a business card that you can staple in your Rolodex." The logo, a strong graphic symbol for the creative firm, is highly visible in all of Levy Creative Management's collateral. "All of our materials create a cohesive and consistent image within our industry. Every marketing piece that leaves our office has our logo and our Web site, and they all coordinate," comments artist representative Sari Levy. "There's a consistency that clients acknowledge and appreciate."

When it comes to promotion, the youthful, eclectic, and happening group is not afraid to explore new and innovative ways to deliver their message. "You can promote yourself in a plethora of ways now, and it certainly doesn't need to be in a brochure format. There are endless opportunities to expand beyond what was once considered typical," says Levy. "We are extremely open-minded when it comes to direct mail and have thus come up with ideas such as games, flip cards, CD-ROMs, DVDs, videos, catalogs, brochures, and more." Levy Creative Management's internationally recognized artists cover a broad spectrum of markets, from movie sets, props, posters, and promotions to editorial, publishing, and advertising work.

In a marketplace that speaks to reduced budgets and limited resources, creatives are doing all they can to make sure that their promotions are as effective as they can be before they are delivered. A lot more time is spent on mock-ups and analyzing just how recipients will read and use what is produced.

FIRM: LEVY CREATIVE MANAGEMENT, LLC

CREATIVE DIRECTOR: MIRKO ILIĆ

DESIGNERS: MIRKO ILIĆ AND HEATH HINEGARDNER

ILLUSTRATION: DAVID COOPER, ALAN DINGMAN, SHANE EVANS, THOMAS FLUHARTY, MAX GRAFE, KRIS HARGIS, JENNY LADEN, TIM OKAMURA, ROBERTO PARADA, LAUREN REDNISS, OREN SHERMAN, DOUG STRUTHERS, AND JONATHAN WEINER

PRINTING: ROB-WIN PRESS, INC.

MANUFACTURER: IMPACT IMAGES (CLEAR BAGS)

BEST IF USED NO LATER THAN NOV 93

WE FOUND THIS ON YOUR ADVERTISING.
CALL US FOR A FRESH BATCH.

Eventually, every sales promotion becomes stale.
And every print campaign loses its fizz.
But don't let them get too outdated.
Call Grafik before it all goes sour.

For more than 20 years,
we've been restocking the region's
most notable marketing departments
with piping hot creative.

Call Lance Wain today at 703.299.4515.
Time is running out.

· WWW.GRAFIK.COM

DANGER! RISK OF SHOCK!

PREPARE YOURSELF.
OUR CREATIVE CAN BE SOMEWHAT JOLTING.

EXPERIENCE GRAFIK

EXPERIENCE G GRAFIK

PREVENTS HAIR LOSS

DEVELOPING AN INTERACTIVE WEB SITE
DOESN'T HAVE TO BE STRESSFUL.

Believe it or not, you really can
create a robust web presence
without a lot of trauma.
Fact is, Grafik helps businesses
and organizations do it everyday.

Call Lance Wain at 703.299.4515.
Lose your troubles – not your hair.

· WWW.GRAFIK.COM

DON'T LET YOUR MARKETING FALL INTO
INEXPERIENCED HANDS.

You're busy. You're rushed.
You're under a lot of pressure.
In short, you have no time for whiny kids.

So why not talk to the
seasoned professionals at Grafik,
the marketing firm that's been providing
adult supervision for more than 20 years.

Call Lance Wain today at 703.299.4515.
It truly is the most mature thing you can do.

· WWW.GRAFIK.COM

KEEP AWAY FROM CHILDREN

Copywriting, which once played second fiddle to design, has become an integral and vital part of the creative process. Most firms now see it as the foundation from which a promotion is built—and rightly so.

just teasing

Looking for a creative way to develop new business, Grafik chose direct mail as the perfect medium to capture the attention of their audience: marketing VPs. "Our primary objective was to create a campaign of mailers that not only spoke directly to the clients' needs but also showed how we could help them solve their most difficult challenges," says creative director and designer David Collins. "We thought it would be fun to do a promotional series around the warning labels you find on products—the expiration date on food, prescription medication warnings, etc. They are common in everyday life, yet appealing as a short, straightforward means of communication." To keep the effort simple and cost-effective, the design team developed a series of two-paneled, wafer-sealed self-mailers to carry their message. Each piece was printed in three PMS colors plus black—a palette taken from Grafik's existing brand identity. To provide visual interest, attention-getting labels were hand-applied slightly askew to each self-mailer. Prospects received one piece every week for four weeks.

The first mailer that was sent shed light on the firm's experience. The teaser "Keep Away from Children" tapped into people's innate desire to protect their young. Hence, this mailer got opened. Inside, the piece warned prospective clients not to let their marketing fall into inexperienced hands and positioned Grafik as the seasoned choice. The second mailer, with the key line "Best If Used No Later Than Nov. 93," focused on the firm's advertising capabilities. Because the date was so old, the recipient was compelled to open the piece to find out what

was so outdated. Inside, they discovered it was their advertising. Grafik then boasted their ability to offer a fresh perspective. The third mailer got itself opened by claiming to prevent hair loss, a popular concern for many. Its slant was to focus on the firm's new media capabilities, stating that Web site development doesn't have to be stressful. The forth and final mailer, entitled "Danger! Risk of Shock!" was a three-paneled, letter-folded piece. It contained an interactive CD-ROM of the firm's visually arresting work.

With clearly defined objectives, a carefully crafted strategy that was mindful of the prospective client's needs, and a series of mailers that really captured the attention of its audience, Grafik was able to deliver their message and get the response they were looking for.

FIRM: GRAFIK

CREATIVE DIRECTORS: DAVID COLLINS AND JUDY KIRPICH

DESIGNERS: DAVID COLLINS AND HAL SWETNAM

PRINTING: McARDLE PRINTING COMPANY

interesting
bindings,
fasteners,
and wraps

Bindery has taken on a new look. Creatives are no longer locked into the traditional saddle-stitched, spiral, or perfect bound brochures. From elastics, stitching, and the tying of a cord to magnets, rivets, and screws of all shapes and sizes, new bindings and fasteners are being discovered. Wraps have also come a long way. Air packs, surgical swab pouches, antistatic bags, and injection-molded tubes are just a few ways creatives are packaging their work. Enclosures are being adapted from sources as diverse as the fashion, automotive, medical, and meatpacking industries. "Look at unexpected sources," advises Eleni Chronopoulos of Reebok International Ltd. "Items that are standard in one industry can appear custom-made in another." Marcie Carson of IE Design adds, "The fashion industry, in particular, is a great place to discover unique odds and ends. Grommets, stitching, button and string closures, ribbons, and wraps are all beautiful binding techniques that have a distinct apparel quality. Occasionally, when I am in need of inspiration, I walk through a fabric store or flip through a fashion magazine. I never know what I might find!" Exploring outside the traditional venues for unconventional bindings, fasteners, and wraps opens the door for new approaches and possibilities.

When searching for alternative solutions, allow yourself to be inspired and excited by even the most inconsequential things. Be sensually open and curious to what surrounds you every day, and you will discover new ways to solve old problems such as bindery. "It's just a matter of being observant," offers illustrator Barbara Lipp. "Someone I know described it as caressing the details of life."

creative
intelligence

The folder that packages all the materials is made of a durable substrate called Lexan. On the back, four rubber automotive joints are placed in die-cut holes to hold the piece together. Round magnets, adhered by hot glue, aid in closing the piece securely. Embossed circles act as guides to ensure proper positioning of the magnets. The business card is uniquely imprinted with the contact person's thumbprint on one side and a simulated magnetic strip on the other. The logo is derived from a 1950s filing cabinet that has steel label holders on the front of each drawer. When placed inside the holder, the label drops down slightly, cutting off the name a bit on the bottom. This look is graphically portrayed in the dossier logo.

Dossiercreative was looking to expand their market and services by repositioning themselves as a full-service branding company. They began their challenge by embarking on an extensive renaming project supplemented by a new identity package. "We started by changing our name to dossier, which means amassing information or intelligence on a subject or a person," says creative director Don Chisholm. "The concept was derived from thinking about how we have successfully worked with our clients. We use a process of collecting data that we call intelligence gathering." In developing their promotional material, dossiercreative wanted to play up on the intelligence concept by using an espionage-like twist.

To handle the task, the group was divided into several cross-functional teams. Once a comprehensive marketing strategy was in place, the design look-and-feel team took over, attacking the problem from both two-and three-dimensional perspectives. Once the idea was conceptualized, the project moved into the hands of the production and implementation team, which explored the feasibility of the desired design. The result was a well-thought-out, group-inspired, and fully integrated piece.

The Lexan folder, designed to simulate a secret report of sorts, holds the overview brochure, proposal brochure, cover letter, note cards, and a business card. Rubber automotive joints hold the piece together, and earth magnets, glued into position, lightly clamp it shut. The overview brochure and proposal, stochastic printed in four-color process plus PMS warm gray #9, features an artistically altered image of a briefcase on the inside French-folded covers. A satin spot varnish is used throughout. A semitranslucent Lexan sheet, silk-screened with a full coverage of warm gray #9, wraps each uniquely bound piece. Both brochures are visually accented with labels and number codes that also function as tracking devices for follow-up procedures. The letterhead and notecards are held together by grommets and a piece of Lexan—an interesting alternative to the paper clip. The business card is die-cut with a semicircle to tie in the grommets, magnets, and screws applied to the other components. Each card is individually marked with the contact person's unique thumbprint, further playing up the espionage concept. On the front of the card is a gray bar that will someday be replaced by a magnetic strip, allowing selective entrance into the firm. All the materials used in this piece add interest and texture to the industrial-looking package. The entire system was designed to be flexible, allowing for weekly or quarterly updates, as the firm requires.

TECHNICAL TIPS

With the Lexan, you cannot apply too much pressure when embossing or it will begin to stress the material, causing it to flare. Make sure you order enough material to test the stress points properly. If you are producing a brochure with both French-folded pages and standard pages, proper finishing work is integral to the success of a quality-looking piece. To avoid problems, each piece must be assembled before it is trimmed and drilled. The nameplates are a wonderful accent to this clever and engaging package. However, the acid-etching process is difficult to execute consistently. Many plates can be destroyed, leaving black and gray streaks on the metallic surface. It is best not to use this process when large quantities are required.

DO IT FOR LESS

Lexan, a washable and durable signage-based substrate, is expensive. There are other materials available that can deliver just as much or more for less money, such as PVC (0.10). Materialconnexion.com, a service that provides access to material specifications and supplier contact information for a nominal fee, is a great way to search for innovative materials and processes worldwide. Assembling the project internally can also save quite a bit of money. To tackle such a feat, you must develop a working plan—determining all of the necessary equipment, workspace, and storage required before the components are delivered. It is cost-prohibitive to produce a similar package using the same materials for large quantities; stick to a low run if budget is a concern.

The overview brochure, wrapped with a Lexan cover, highlights the firm's mission statement, operations, branding services, five-step working process, case studies, and diversified portfolio. It is bound with an acid-etched, stainless steel nameplate and a combination of stainless steel screws mixed with ³/₈-inch (1-cm) aluminum Chicago screw backs—both special-ordered in the right depth. French-folded pages cover the brochure and divide the subject matter, giving weight to the overall piece. The letterhead is held together by grommets with a sampling of the Lexan material to make a connection to the rest of the package. The industrial-looking brochure is given to prospective clients. The proposal brochure, sent to existing clients, is bound with grommets, and the dossier logo is blind-embossed at the top and on the back of the Lexan wrap. It is used to hold proposals, case studies, and portfolio samples.

The notecards, which echo the graphics and key messaging from the overview brochure, are held together by grommets. A sampling of the Lexan material is brought in for visual continuity. The notecards are sent with the packet as a teaser or can be used as thank-you cards.

FIRM: DOSSIERCREATIVE

CREATIVE DIRECTOR: DON CHISHOLM

DESIGNER: MATTI CROSS

PHOTOGRAPHY: VERVE PHOTOGRAPHIC AND
   TONY HURLEY PHOTOGRAPHY

PRINTER AND BINDERY: HEMLOCK PRINTERS

SPECIAL TECHNIQUES: WESTERN NAMEPLATES

MANUFACTURER: PACIFIC FASTENERS

1

3

2

so you're getting married

The elegant keepsake promotion is presented inside a custom-designed box eloquently detailed with a silver foil–stamped logo. Inside the box, lies a side-sewn brochure accented by a silver grommet and hand-dyed ribbon. Candles are used as add-ons and serve as symbols of warmth and hope during this special time in one's life.

Good Gracious! Events, specialists in event planning and custom catering, wanted to have a signature piece to promote their wedding services. "When I sat down with the owner, it was clear that a typical white-and-gold bridal package would not suffice," remembers creative director and designer Marcie Carson. "Good Gracious's wedding events are magical, colorful, and romantic, and we really needed to convey that feeling in the piece."

To communicate just the right message, the promotion had to exhibit an artistic, almost signaturelike, quality with a keen attention for detail. It was important that the piece seem like a keepsake, something that signified the beginning of a beautiful experience to come. To make the piece more giftlike, both the designer and client agreed that candles, symbols of hope and life, were the perfect supportive elements. "We started with three candles—deep rust, magenta, and orange—avoiding the expected whites and creams," shares Carson. "We then began to look at box options and different coverings for the exterior, like bookcloth and handmade papers." The box had to be not only stunning but also durable enough to mail without looking bulky. To bring out the colors in the candles, the custom-manufactured box was wrapped with rust bookcloth and lined with handmade paper. A silver foil logo added detail to the exterior lid. Once the right look and feel of the box was in place, the designer began developing a brochure and identity system to bring the whole promotion together.

To showcase the company's extensive array of wedding services, a stunning brochure was created with many signature touches. The stitched binding, silver grommet, hand-dyed silk ribbon tie, and letterpress printing all contribute to the artistic quality of the piece. Throughout, key words like *promise*, *bond*, *savor*, *unity*, and *bliss* help position Good Gracious! Events as the company to make your wedding memorable from beginning to end. The warm and inviting wedding ensemble is sent as a self-mailer with a cover letter and business card. The entire package exudes the elegance and romance that most brides look for in their special day.

TECHNICAL TIPS

When creating a custom box such as this one, it is important to work closely with your vendors to be sure they clearly understand your vision. If you choose to use the box as a self-mailer, do a test mailing. The test mailing for this project showed that dividers were needed inside the box to prevent the candles from rolling around and chipping.

3

The promotional ensemble is designed as a self-mailer with the addition of a custom mailing label. The letterpress and offset-printed brochure juxtaposes beautiful floral patterns, which come to life with a tinted varnish, against copy that is warm, inviting, and reassuring.

Each package comes with a personalized note on custom-designed stationery. The letterhead, envelope, and business card make a connection with the rest of the promotion by incorporating the rust, silver, and tan color scheme and by picking up on the beautifully illustrated floral pattern.

1

CLIENT: GOOD GRACIOUS! EVENTS

FIRM: [I]E DESIGN

CREATIVE DIRECTOR AND DESIGNER: MARCIE CARSON

ILLUSTRATION: CYA NELSON

PRINTING: ROADRUNNER PRESS
(BROCHURE AND STATIONERY SYSTEM), AND AMES LETTERPRESS

BINDERY: C & S SALES (STITCHING AND GROMMET)

MANUFACTURER: C & S SALES (BOX)

2

team players

To attract high-profile clients to their firm, Atom Design wanted to developed an image-building brochure with a strong business message that focused on creating partnerships, developing innovative solutions, and achieving results. "There is a lot of creative work out there, but it often doesn't meet the client's brief," observes creative director David Springford. "Our message is to convey that we are a young, approachable team who believe function is equal to form. Our creative and approachable nature is often appealing to large corporations, who can see the benefit in working with a smaller and more personal agency."

To ignite the process, a creative brief was formed, and the design team went to work. The result was an inviting brochure, an introduction of sorts. "We wouldn't expect you to want to work with a company you knew nothing about," the brochure copy details. "So, before you get involved with us, we'd like to tell you a bit about ourselves." The copy is warm, friendly, and flows from one page to the next to tell the company's story. Each spread delivers a brand-building message, whether for the design firm itself or for its clients. The dot patterns, symbolic of atoms, on the left-hand pages work in conjunction with the text and imagery to send a subtle message. "We wanted people to see that there is thought and depth behind the brochure," notes Springford. "Some clients pick up on it the first time and others the second or third."

On the cover, the firm's atom identity mark is interestingly portrayed. A small, centrally located die-cut hole reveals the logo through the brightly colored tissue-paper wrap underneath. The 28-page promotion is uniquely bound with an elastic band, which allows the piece to be expanded over time. The elastic is pulled taught, stitched, and wrapped over two half-circle cuts to keep it in place. The simple but elegant cover, unusual binding, use of vivid color, and the French-folded inside pages all add value and interest to the overall piece, leaving a lasting impression in the minds of many. "We wanted the brochure to be interesting, a little different, and precious," offers Springford. "Our aim was to provide prospective clients with an overall impression of our company and the varied work we produce." The piece is sent to prospective clients in a flat cardboard box that is folded and securely sealed with white cloth tape. "We are very proud of the result. We usually get a wow from people viewing it for the first time," concludes Springford. "It also allows us the opportunity to do something that clients fear. When they see the results, they may feel more comfortable pushing their boundaries."

TECHNICAL TIPS

To develop a promotional piece that is outside the norm, you have to do research. Start with the intent and find a solution that best suits that problem, being open to searching areas outside the graphic design industry. Play, experiment, and keep an ongoing file of readily available materials and techniques.

1

The clean and understated cover is accented by the vivid color in the elastic binding and tissue-paper wrap, revealed through a small, centrally located die-cut hole. Throughout the brochure, each spread cleverly uses imagery, copy, and graphics to communicate key points to the audience.

2

The series of portfolio case studies helps show the range and diversity of work of which Atom Design is capable. Key words assist in highlighting how the design firm is able to work with clients to produce innovative solutions that achieve results. Each photograph is taken on client premises by the staff.

1

2

FIRM: ATOM DESIGN

CREATIVE DIRECTOR: DAVID SPRINGFORD

DESIGNERS: WILL PRICE, HELEN EVANS, AND DAVID SPRINGFORD

ILLUSTRATION: ATOM DESIGN TEAM

PHOTOGRAPHY: DAVID SPRINGFORD

PRINTING: ARC COLOURPRINT LTD.

SPECIAL TECHNIQUES: ARC COLOURPRINTER LTD. (DIE-CUTTING)

MANUFACTURERS: UK SEWING SERVICES (ELASTIC AND STITCHING), CITY LITHO LTD. (BOX), AND WRAPOLOGY LTD. (TISSUE)

The incriminating promotion comes in a black semigloss standard-size box adorned with an embossed metallic self-adhesive label that reveals the concept "Ten Years Hard Labour." Inside, a prison beanie, chocolate phone, and visitor's pass are added for visual support. All of the items sit securely inside a die-cut insert made of embossed Chequer-flute board that gives the appearance of prison cells. The promotion is sealed with a fluorescent orange sticker and hand-delivered to existing clients.

With ten years under their belt, the small New Zealand–based design firm wanted to celebrate. But what to do and how to do it was the question that creative director and designer Alexander Lloyd faced. To tackle the problem at hand, the creative firm immediately started brainstorming, looking for an unusual way to express their decade of hard work and business success. "I was trying to think of an angle and the phrase *Ten Years Hard Labour* seemed to pop out," says Lloyd. " To give the promotion a humorous twist, I came up with the idea of presenting myself as a convict."

The lead piece, a thirty-two-page, self-cover booklet and portfolio presentation, sheds insight into the mind and work of this ten-year graphic offender. "It begins so subtly, so insignificantly, you hardly realize you're getting involved in the world of graphic design. It might start with a logo here or a flyer there, maybe an advert or two, and before you know it, you're hooked," Lloyd cleverly writes. "And after a while you can't help yourself but spend countless hours studying the packaging at the supermarket or making covert brochure runs at visitor information centers—and fonts, don't get me started." Such confessions of a condemned lifer in the field of graphic design add an element of humor and interest to the portfolio display. The offset-printed piece closes with a section called The Casualties, which explores some of the ideas that have never seen the light of day—"forgotten designs in the minefield of graphic design," as Lloyd puts it.

The tongue-in-cheek promotion comes in a black box sealed with a fluorescent orange approval sticker from the pseudo Department of Graphic Design, Corrections, and Incarcerations. For the recipient, breaking the seal symbolizes acceptance of the enclosed graphic material, ten years in the making. An embossed metallic self-adhesive label mounted on the cover presents the concept. Inside lies the supporting cast of characters in this criminal escapade: a machine-embroidered black beanie, a visitor's tag, and a chocolate cell phone. The tag, printed in-house, is laminated with clear contact paper and trimmed to size. A clip completes the effect. The chocolate cell phone, bought at a local department store, was customized by replacing the backing and trimming the piece slightly. The biggest challenge, believe it or not, was removing the stubborn price tags.

By positioning himself as a graphic design junkie serving time for his serial offences, the designer was able to create a memorable and quite entertaining promotion to celebrate his first decade in business. With such dedication and creative ingenuity, it looks like Lloyd is in for another ten years. Parole denied!

TECHNICAL TIPS

If you are going to reproduce your portfolio in a booklet format, print more than you need so you can continue to hand them out throughout the year. The unit cost will be cheaper and you will avoid having to send out your limited supply of samples and tear sheets when clients request them. When creating a die-cut insert, make sure to account for the thickness of the paper. The insert must fit just right—not so tight that it buckles and not so loose that it slides out. When in doubt, make a mockup in the actual stock you want to use. Always contact your vendors for advice. When ordering custom-designed embroidery, you must supply camera-ready artwork rather than digital files.

DO IT FOR LESS

The die-cut insert is made with an expensive stock that comes embossed, but a simple, off-the-shelf paper can be used to save money. For further savings, a lot of printing, collating, bindery, and assembling can be done in-house.

The thirty-two-page, self-cover booklet, bound with an Acco 875 fastener, presents the design firm's criminal dedication to the field in a humorous and entertaining manner.

Within the promotional booklet, the design firm displays their best work. A range of projects is shown, including label and package design, business collateral, corporate identity, and branding, with a strong emphasis on logo development. At the end, four pages are dedicated to ideas that have never seen the light of day. The pages are conveniently scored so they turn easily within the tightly bound book.

1

2

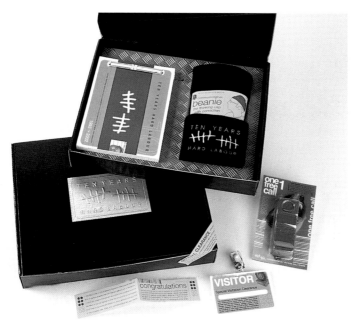

3

FIRM: LLOYD'S GRAPHIC DESIGN AND COMMUNICATION

CREATIVE DIRECTOR AND DESIGNER: ALEXANDER LLOYD

ILLUSTRATION: ALEXANDER LLOYD

PHOTOGRAPHY: ALEXANDER LLOYD AND JAAP VAN DER STOEL

PRINTING: BLENHEIM PRINTING COMPANY (BOOKLET) AND
    KNIGHT PRINT LTD. (BACKING FOR CHOCOLATE PHONE)

SPECIAL TECHNIQUES: NEWMAN GRAPHICS (HAT EMBROIDERY)

MANUFACTURERS: BERICA MARKETING (BOX AND BOX INSERT),
    ACCO NEW ZEALAND LTD. (BOOKLET BINDING),
    AND CORPORATE EXPRESS (TAG CLIP)

picturing words

Every year, Pentagram creates a little keepsake for clients, friends, and colleagues. The thought-provoking and intellectually stimulating gift is meant as a diversion during the crazy year-end months when everyone is overly bombarded with holiday messaging. To stand out from the crowd, Pentagram's signature booklets never refer to the season. This year was no different.

Inspired by the idea of wordplay, creative director and designer John McConnell chose to explore the game of crossword, giving it an innovative twist. Instead of using written clues to generate answers for the puzzle, he devised pictures or visual clues. Throughout the minibooklet, images—from Andy Warhol's Campbell's Soup Can to the bee from Paul Rand's famous reworking of the IBM logo—stimulate and challenge the viewer. Because of its universal appeal, the highly pictorial format was the perfect platform for Pentagram's international audience, as it utilizes a language that is not only familiar but also easy to understand despite cultural and language differences. As stated in the introduction, "Here's a crossword without any words for clues, just pictures instead. It's probably the biggest breakthrough in the history of making up crosswords since the cryptic crossword appeared in London's *Saturday Westminster* in 1925. It could even be as momentous as the very first crossword puzzle, which was created by Arthur Wynne from Liverpool and published in the *New York World* on December 21, 1913. With this acute sense of history, we draw a close to the twentieth century and the second millennium."

The ingenious idea had to be presented in a format that expressed its historical roots, so McConnell looked toward traditional bookmaking techniques. An exposed stitched bindery adheres an extended cover to three insert additions, making for an intimate twelve-page booklet. The highly textured black surface is accented, front and back, by white foil stamping that punctures the surface like an old letterpress. The simple but highly sophisticated piece was mailed in a white envelope to keep within the high-contrast color scheme. The only point of contact was a listing of Pentagram's worldwide offices on the back. It just goes to show how the simplest ideas can often be the most effective.

TECHNICAL TIPS

Small formats with interesting touches make a promotion more intimate and personal. Foil stamping can provide a nice, almost letterpress-like, effect. As an added bonus, an interesting graphic impression is created on the opposite side, something to incorporate into your overall design. Working with a colored stock is advantageous over printing a solid when you want even coverage that will not crack when folded.

DO IT FOR LESS

If you have more time than money to spend, read up on handmade books. Researching historical techniques and formats can add a vintage flair to your promotion. Reference sources also give step-by-step instructions on stitched bindery, ties, and wraps in an array of formats.

1

1

The white foil-stamped black cover sets the stage for a pictorial crossword game. The piece opens to a cleverly worded introduction that describes its historical significance.

2

Inside the stitch-bound booklet, well-known icons and universal imagery serve as visual clues to a white foil-stamped puzzle that unfolds in the back.

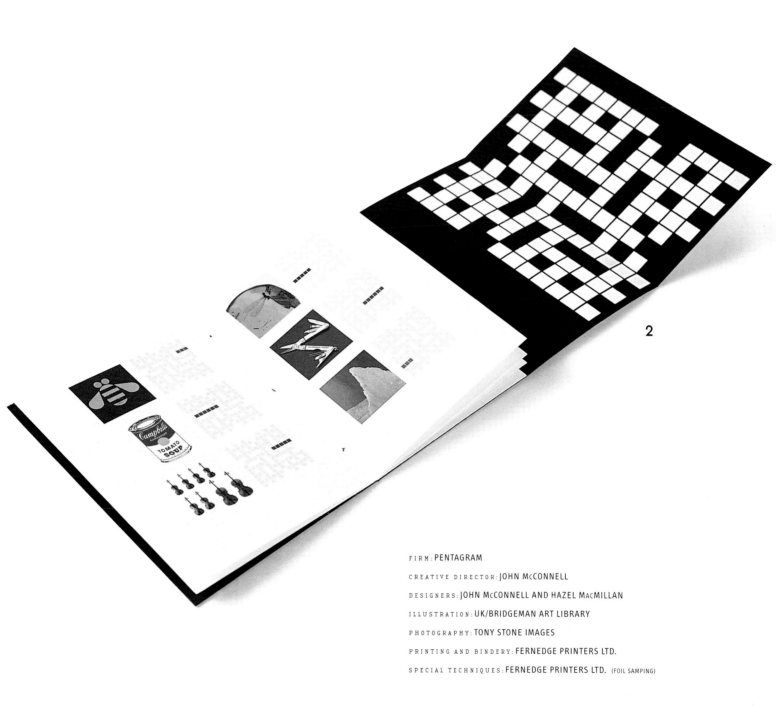

2

FIRM: PENTAGRAM

CREATIVE DIRECTOR: JOHN McCONNELL

DESIGNERS: JOHN McCONNELL AND HAZEL MacMILLAN

ILLUSTRATION: UK/BRIDGEMAN ART LIBRARY

PHOTOGRAPHY: TONY STONE IMAGES

PRINTING AND BINDERY: FERNEDGE PRINTERS LTD.

SPECIAL TECHNIQUES: FERNEDGE PRINTERS LTD. (FOIL SAMPING)

# of form and function

After a rebranding effort, ASK & Company made some interesting discoveries. The rebranding process sparked not only a name change but also a redirection for the company, now called Capsule. "Capsule is an environment where people and ideas come together around a process that results in understanding and insight," comments managing principal Aaron Keller. "We use the name to reference exploration, finding new ways of doing business as a design firm." To communicate their metamorphosis to the business community, the design firm needed a promotion that not only announced the name change but also expressed the new approach to design.

To develop just the right device to deliver their message, the design team did extensive exploratory research, analyzing the competitive landscape with respect to messaging, communications collateral, and overall brand development. They also sought secondary sources from the Internet, the local library, and a day trip to the space exhibit at the Art Institute of Chicago. Their efforts resulted in a promotion that helped communicate Capsule's process and approach to design—explore, discover, and evolve—in an interesting and intriguing way.

The tactile materials, bindery, and all of the accents offered an intriguing mix of contemporary and historical references. "We used the metallic paper to reflect a futuristic view of exploration," says Keller, "and the blotter paper and letterpress printing to reflect the historic craft of our business." To pique curiosity, the simple, yet effective, promotion was wrapped inside a beautifully embossed bellyband. "It requires someone to tear into the piece to find out what is inside," explains Keller. "That simple interaction starts the discovery process."

The piece is both aesthetically pleasing and multifunctional. Each page within the screw-bound brochure can be easily ripped out and converted into a coaster, giving the promotional endeavor an extended life. The die-cut accents are also structurally functional and visually interesting. The two indents on the top and bottom help secure the bellyband in place, while the curvilinear die-cut shapes serve as artistic detail that complements each page. "Combining functionality and aesthetics into one communications piece is a way of thinking beyond the message," adds Keller. "This promotion exemplifies the quality of our work without specifically providing a bullet point list of services. We used it to bring our firm to the next level of visibility."

TECHNICAL TIPS

When letterpress printing on nontraditional materials, be mindful of the limitations, and be involved in every aspect of the process to ensure the final deliverable is what you want. Die-cutting a thick stock requires special attention and should be thoroughly tested in advance. If you choose to print on metallic papers, make sure you allow enough time for the inks to dry.

Curious Galvanized 92-lb. cover, a metallic paper, gave the promotion's wraparound cover an intriguing space-age quality. The screwposts that bind the piece together are positioned to maintain overall stability when detaching each page from the base to create coasters. The embossed bellyband that surrounds the piece helps spark curiosity and interest, while the exterior packaging, a silver, heat-sealed, static-free bag, plays up the theme of exploration and discovery. Two die-cut marks on either side of the bag make it easy to open.

Inside the piece, thick, highly textured blotter paper is letterpress-printed, giving it a handcrafted quality. Silver ink creates a visual connection with the metallic paper and silver packaging. Each page within the piece can be transformed into a coaster by simply tearing at the perforated edge.

1

2

FIRM: CAPSULE

CREATIVE DIRECTOR: BRIAN ADDUCCI

DESIGNER: DAN BAGGENSTOSS

PHOTOGRAPHY: NASA

PRINTING AND BINDERY: DIVERSIFIED GRAPHICS, INC.

MANUFACTURER: ULINE (SILVER BAGS)

everyday
life:
abstracted

Nick Veasey, known for his abstract vision of everyday life, wanted a promotion that would attract the attention of both European and U.S. buyers. "Photography is a competitive business. You have to stand out somehow. Many promotions are thrown away or kept in some file that never gets looked at," admits Veasey. "I wanted something that people would keep and remember." To create a promotion that really deviated from the norm, Veasey employed the assistance of creative director and designer Zoe Scutts. "We talked things through over a period of weeks, showing each other found objects and looking through books," says Veasey. "Zoe wanted it to be small, while I wanted larger pictures. But she was right, because my clients get to see my pictures bigger when they call in for my portfolio or check the Web site. The piece works because of its size." Working collaboratively the two came up with a promotion that was as distinctive as the photography it highlighted.

To bring in an element of surprise, a commercial blister pack was chosen as the perfect packaging solution; it created the unexpected, yet still utilitarian, feel the team was looking for. "We both find beauty in the everyday," notes Veasey. "Actually, we got the blister pack idea from buying some screws in a store." Inside the transparent pack, selected works from the portfolio of photographer Nick Veasey are revealed. From page to page, abstractly interpreted slice-of-life shots were positioned against x-rayed still lives and figurative subject matter. Each custom die-cut page was matte laminated to tie in the look and feel of the outer plastic packaging as well as to protect the photographic promotion from wear and tear. (Originally, the team wanted to print on plastic, but research showed that the process was too expensive; in addition, it would not have served the promotion well because the printing quality is far inferior.) The piece was bound together by a chain, with a joining clasp applied over both ends to keep it shut. The chain not only provides easy access to the diverse array of images but also adds interest to the overall piece.

The pocket-sized promotion attracted attention on many fronts. "It is difficult to create something that will get noticed by the most visually aware people in the world," admits Veasey. "If you bring a bit of the other world into the offices of these people, it makes them stop and think for a second." The miniportfolio served as an introduction to new clients and a reminder to existing clients of the extraordinary work of photographer Nick Veasey.

TECHNICAL TIPS

When developing direct mail, you need to create something that is not only thought-provoking but also instantly grabs the recipient's attention, motivating them to look inside and further participate in the overall messaging. To create distinction, explore alternative materials, formats, and techniques. Suppliers can be found everywhere; the Internet is the best place to start your search.

1

2

The minipromotion is housed in a transparent plastic blister pack to create distinction and attract attention. Small address labels are affixed to the back, and the piece is mailed to prospective art buyers in Europe and the United States without any additional packaging.

Inside the blister pack is a chain-bound promotion featuring the work of photographer Nick Veasey. Each custom die-cut page varies from abstract imagery to interesting objects and figures that have been exposed in an x-rayed fashion. Each custom die-cut card is printed in four-color process on 350-gram Hello Silk stock.

1

FIRM: UNTITLED

CREATIVE DIRECTOR AND DESIGNER: ZOE SCUTTS

PHOTOGRAPHY: NICK VEASEY

PRINTING AND BINDERY: ONE EXCEPTION

MANUFACTURERS: MACPAC (BLISTER PACKS) AND ZINCO (CHAINS)

2

collaborative endeavors

Through collaborative endeavors, creatives are reexamining the fundamental methodology whereby they promote and do business, making a difference in their work, the industry, and the world at large. Under a group dynamic, each contributor brings his or her insight, creativity, and know-how to the table, offering a fresh perspective on problem solving. Their combined efforts, energy, and wisdom lift the group to a new level. "When collaborating, you give your ultimate best because there is a heightened responsibility to do so," shares Deb Koch of Red Canoe. "Working with someone new challenges me personally to rise to higher levels." Group-sponsored initiatives create an environment conducive to the pursuit of new ideas, encouraging participants to grow in ways they would not have individually.

When embarking on a group endeavor, it is important to be organized from the start. It is essential to set ground rules and to produce a detailed creative brief, outlining the project's intent, overall theme, and working specifications. A solid timeline, detailing individual responsibilities and due dates, will also prove helpful in keeping each participant on track. To ensure everything runs smoothly, it is beneficial to have someone in charge of project management, coordinating all of the many threads. "Collaboration among independent, passionate, and strong-willed people will naturally entail opposing opinions, so anticipate and expect some healthy conflict," Koch advises. "Establish up front precisely how problems will be handled and who will make the final decision for each aspect of the project. It might seem like a tedious process, but don't underestimate its necessity." Most important, it is essential for each participant to maintain an open mind and a clear channel of communications. Trust and mutual respect among all involved is vital as well.

By working collaboratively, the partners at Pentagram Design have been able to explore avenues far more outstanding than any one member would have had the budget, time, or resources for. Given their international network, each office can offer clients a broad range of services and expertise, from architecture, interior, and exhibition design to graphic and product design. Although they are a partnership, each of the highly recognized designers works independently as the head of his or her autonomous group. This infrastructure helps maintain administrative control among the group while allowing for a consistent, single point of contact for the client. "It also gives us the efficiency to take on very small jobs and permits each partner to stay fresh and involved with clients and projects," offers partner Michael Bierut. "When we collaborate, it is generally because two or more of the partners have skills or interests that can be brought to bear on a specific project." When shared skills are needed, various partners draw on the resources of the whole organization to realize the project, an incredible benefit that makes Pentagram unique in the marketplace. Through the experience, knowledge, and resources of the group, each partner has been able to expand on his or her own talents and abilities, reaching new heights as a result.

When you chose to collaborate, you begin to build relationships and connections to resources that can prove valuable down the road. Designer Milton Glaser, who has cultivated many contacts over the course of his career, can now use his talents and ingenuity to pursue causes he believes in, inspiring others to follow suit. "If you are in the communications business, you have a special opportunity to use your skills for some kind of public good. You can't only be involved with selling products, at least not in my view," he says.

"Every once in a while, you should take the opportunity to act." When you are pursuing a self-initiated project, certainly one that is not profit driven, it is difficult to create a point of entry into the marketplace. "Everything is driven by money. When there isn't sponsorship behind something, there is no effective means of distribution," Glaser adds. "You have to find some connective tissue to enter into the culture." Without an institutional contact or underlying support system, it is difficult to get the necessary visibility to make something effective enough to enter the public consciousness. "No matter how good the idea is, you are barking at the Moon without the personal connections that enable the idea to penetrate," comments Glaser. "You have to hook into the media, whether it is getting someone to sponsor a subway poster or getting radio or TV coverage. Also, the message has to be of sufficient interest intrinsically, so that you will get people to pay attention." By establishing relationships with people outside of your discipline, you gain access to the bloodstream of the market. Having media contacts, support from vendors, and established relationships with institutions can be invaluable when pursuing initiatives, especially those that are far more expansive than the mere selling of products or services.

It takes a lot of effort from dedicated people to launch a group-inspired endeavor. But for those willing to share their talent, cross existing boundaries, and try new ways of working, collaboration can be profoundly rewarding. Furthermore, once a group effort is successfully realized, it provides leverage for other endeavors, opening up new opportunities for all involved. Creatives choosing to work collaboratively are truly establishing new pathways in what is possible when it comes to promotion.

collaborations that educate

Since 1975, the partners at Pentagram have designed and produced a series of booklets, called *Pentagram Papers*, that cover a wide range of topics— sometimes controversial and other times quite entertaining. The educational emphasis is on exposing the masses to the extraordinary. To maintain consistency, each book utilizes a similar format, a wraparound jacket printed in solid black with a dull varnish on the outside and a gloss varnish on the inside. The books are distributed to clients, colleagues, friends, educational institutions, and libraries as a way to share ideas and inspiring subject matter with the industry. "Of all the things we publish to promote the partnership, the *Pentagram Papers* is the most enthusiastically received," shares partner Michael Bierut. "They never show examples of our work but, rather, examples of our interests and how we think." Through the efforts of the Pentagram partnership, an array of thought-provoking and intellectually stimulating books have entered the design community, sending the partnership into the limelight as innovators in a league all their own.

Many of the books reveal fascinating places and subject matter that would otherwise remain untouched. For instance, *Pentagram Papers 27: Nifty Places, The Australian Rural Mailbox*, is truly visual eye candy portraying the most bizarre adaptations to the mailbox, from old banged-up refrigerators to recycled milk churns and rusty oil drums. The audacity just screams for publication. "One of the most visible demonstrations of Aussie individuality and inventiveness, bordering on art on the one hand and environmental vandalism on the other, is the rural mailbox," says author Cal Swann. "They are all an expression of freedom and the rights of individuals to choose." Another good example is *Pentagram Papers 30: Neon-Lit, Kidney-Shaped, Low-Rent, Flat-Roofed, Doo-Wop Commercial Architecture, or, Learning from Wildwood, New Jersey*. The title is a long but accurate description of a series of photographs taken by Dorothy Kresz during her vacations to New Jersey's south shore. "Wildwood is an ossifying, urban, challenging place with a bad neighborhood or two, bars and nightclubs, drug problems, and a 26 percent unemployment rate," says author Jonathan van Meter. "It's a bit grubby and wonderfully tacky, lit with neon signs and dotted with big plastic palm trees in lieu of actual greenery." Many claim that the kitschy architecture and eye-catching urban signage is one of the strongest concentrations of midcentury commercial structures in the world. It is no wonder that partner Michael Bierut was so drawn to it.

Other books are inspired by an experience or unique project that comes along. Such was the case in 1995, when Pentagram partner John Rushworth was asked by the Savoy Group of Hotels and Restaurants to develop a new identity for its prestigious and historic luxury hotels. Awestruck by the architecture and the lighting, Rushworth and his design team created *Pentagram Papers 29: Savoy Lights*. The Savoy, located in London's West End, opened its doors in 1899. Creator Richard d'Oyly Carte, a man of the theater, had exquisite taste and a keen understanding of how lighting creates ambience and mood. The lighting, both public and private, remains revolutionary even today.

Pentagram's most recent publishing endeavor originated in Pentagram partner Kit Hinrichs's lucky find at an antiquarian book fair. *Hinagata*, a kimono pattern book from 1899, was so beautifully constructed and illuminated with wood block printed imagery that it led the designer to investigate its roots. Yoshiko I. Wada, a fellow at the Center for Japanese Studies at the University of California, Berkeley, was brought in to assist in the search. The rich and graphic kimono designs are quite compelling and visually luscious. It is easy to see why Hinrichs found them fascinating enough to share. Shown are just four of the most recent of the thirty-one books in the *Pentagram Papers* series.

FIRM: PENTAGRAM DESIGN

DESIGNERS: DAVID HILLMAN (PENTAGRAM PAPERS 27), JOHN RUSHWORTH
(PENTAGRAM PAPERS 29), MICHAEL BIERUT (PENTAGRAM PAPERS 30),
AND KIT HINRICHS (PENTAGRAM PAPERS 31)

PARTICIPANTS: CAL SWANN (PENTAGRAM PAPERS 27), GRAHAM VICKERS
(PENTAGRAM PAPERS 29), JONATHAN VAN METER (PENTAGRAM PAPERS 30),
YOSHIKO I. WADA, AND DELPHINE HIRASUNA (PENTAGRAM PAPERS 31)

PHOTOGRAPHY: CAL SWANN (PENTAGRAM PAPERS 27), PHIL SAYER (PENTAGRAM
PAPERS 29), DOROTHY KRESZ (PENTAGRAM PAPERS 30), AND TERRY HEFFERNAN
(PENTAGRAM PAPERS 31)

PRINTING AND BINDERY: ALDERSON BROTHERS PRINTERS LIMITED
(PENTAGRAM PAPERS 27), GAVIN MARTIN ASSOCIATES (PENTAGRAM PAPERS 29),
THE CAMPBELL GROUP (PENTAGRAM PAPERS 30), AND ANDERSON
LITHOGRAPH (PENTAGRAM PAPERS 31)

FIRM: RED CANOE

CREATIVE DIRECTOR: DEB KOCH

DESIGNER: CAROLINE KAVANAGH

ILLUSTRATION: KATHERINE DUNN

PRINTING: STUDIO INK (SILK-SCREEN ON WOOD)

   AND EPSON INKJET PRINTER (BOOKLET, BUSINESS CARD, AND WRAPPING PAPER)

MANUFACTURERS: PAPER MART (NATURAL WOOD EXCELSIOR ASPEN WOOD SHAVINGS)

   AND RED CANOE SITE (ACORNS, WOOD SLICES, AND STICKS)

creative collaboration

Creatives are beginning to realize the promotional potential that results when they join forces on a collaborative endeavor. Such was the case when Deb Koch and Caroline Kavanagh, cofounders of Red Canoe, teamed up with illustrator Katherine Dunn. After creating a Web site design for Dunn, the team of creatives realized they had a lot in common. With shared interests and an overlapping client base, they embarked on a dual-functioning promotion that not only enticed prospects to visit and bookmark Dunn's new site but also drew attention to the interactive design and development capabilities of Red Canoe.

To capture the attention of their mostly creative audience, the promotion had to be interesting enough to stand out from the flood of incoming mailers. To develop something that successfully promoted both companies, the design team went back to their shared inspirational source—nature. Dunn's illustrative Web site, which draws a lot of its key components from natural elements, was in perfect tune with the philosophy and mission statement of Red Canoe. To make a familiar connection, the design team went out into their 350 acres of natural woodland and collected many of the elements that appear on the Web site: wood, sticks, and acorns. This made for a very tactile introduction to the Web site's electronic experience. "The concept was to bring dimension and reality to some of the site's elements, enhancing one's sense of the site as a place that one would immediately feel familiar with," offers Koch.

Acorn tops and bottoms were cleaned and glued back together with biodegradable material. The wood and twigs were gathered from fallen tree branches, cut, and sanded to smooth and brighten their surface. To remove moisture, the slices of wood were baked in a conventional oven until perfectly dry. They were later silk-screen-printed with the Web site's URL. The mini-slices of wood served a secondary function as coasters, increasing the longevity of the piece. A little, illustrated storybook with rhythmic sayings and French-folded pages enticed the recipient to visit the newly developed site. To add character and distinction, the minibook was wrapped with a cover stock and uniquely bound with a rubber band and stick. Wood shavings, shaped into a nest, housed the piece. The package was sent in a white box wrapped by a custom-designed sheet accented with the artist's gestural work. The narrative approach, natural materials, and keen attention to detail helped make the piece memorable and the URL (leaves-no-more-than-i-do.com) something worth exploring further.

For the design firm, collaboration is a way to enrich their portfolio and diversify their capabilities. "Besides the new-blood aspect of creative input, each collaborative endeavor reveals new processes that contribute to the flow of the next project, whatever it may be," says Koch. "It allows clients to see skills and talent that go beyond the generally perceived scope of design, creating unique projects and work opportunities." Although you give up a certain amount of personal ownership when collaborating, a project somehow always goes beyond what it otherwise would have because of the contribution of others.

When embarking on a group endeavor, it is important to be organized from the start. It is essential to set ground rules and to produce a detailed creative brief, outlining the project's intent, overall theme, and working specifications. A solid timeline, detailing individual responsibilities and due dates, will also prove helpful in keeping each participant on track.

When you chose to collaborate, you begin to build relationships and connections to resources that can prove valuable down the road.

FIRM: MILTON GLASER, INC.

CREATIVE DIRECTOR AND DESIGNER:
MILTON GLASER

PRINTING: RASCO GRAPHICS, INC. (POSTER)

MANUFACTURER: NC SLATER CORPORATION (BUTTONS)

making a difference

Because of the tragic events of September 11, creatives around the world have become much more introspective, reexamining the purpose and the role they play in society, not only as businesses but also as individuals. In the aftermath, many felt a great deal of loss and uncertainty. The world was forever changed, and nobody knew quite what to do about it. "After 9/11, I got up one morning and I said 'I love New York' isn't complete anymore as a proposition," recalls creative director and designer Milton Glaser. "I realized that my feelings about the city had changed fundamentally. The city was vulnerable making me realize the sense of potential loss similar to when someone is sick and you begin to recognize just how much you love them." Glaser went back to his original "I love New York" design and added the endearing words "more than ever." In addition, a black stain on the lower part of the heart was made in acknowledgment of the destruction in lower Manhattan.

In an attempt to shift social consciousness, the designer asked the School of Visual Arts (SVA), where he lectures, to produce a poster to be distributed around the city by students. The poster was given to merchants for placement in storefront windows. In addition, the poster was positioned within SVA's vast transit advertising in subways in Manhattan and the surrounding boroughs. To expand the concept, Glaser contacted National Public Radio. "I connected with WNYC, and they used the posters to raise money to assist in the restoration of their antenna," says Glaser. "If you sent in a contribution, you got a free poster. They raised $190,000. I was very encouraged by that."

As a way of continuing the momentum, Glaser embarked on a campaign to preempt a war. "I felt we all had to do something about the extraordinary passivity that exists in this country and the lack of demonstrable opposition to the policies of the government," he construes. "One thing I could do was to give people an instrument with which to express their opinions overtly." To encourage social commentary in a visible way, Glaser contacted the *Nation*, proposing a joint venture button initiative that would be advertised in their publication. To lead the initiative, two buttons were designed, respectively reading Dissent Protects Democracy and Preempt the War. It was a tremendous success, leading to another wave of buttons. Leave No CEO Behind, Secrecy Promotes Tyranny, Oil War, and Surveillance Undermines Liberty became the messaging chosen for round two of the Join the Loyal Opposition campaign. Glaser is currently working on yet another initiative, Together for the City We Love. "It seems to me that unless we are conscious of the fact that we are all in this together, we will never recover," he acknowledges. "It is everybody's responsibility to help the city along by withdrawing from the idea of self-interest and personal opportunism that is destroying everything. If we only think about ourselves, the world is completely doomed. I am galvanized by this sense of urgency."

Creatives choosing to work collaboratively are truly establishing new pathways in what is possible when it comes to promotion.

fruitful campaign

Captivating its audience with a piece of trivia, the self-mailer encourages the viewer to open it in search of an answer. Inside is an invitation to the anniversary party and a set of four orange trivia coasters printed on board stock. These are held securely together in a plastic bag that is blindly stapled to an inside fold within the mailer. The stitched bindery adds an interesting accent to the digitally printed and hand-assembled piece.

After four years of doing business as Wolf Creative, president and creative director Damien Wolf wanted to redirect his company, expanding its offerings and services. "Last year I spent a few months really thinking about the direction and redoing the business plan," reflects Wolf. "We needed to redefine our focus more on business communications and marketing strategies." To make a fresh start, Wolf decided a rebranding and name change was appropriate and necessary for his growing business. The question was what to call this new company. Wolf recalls, "About seven years ago, before I started the studio, I pushed some orange seeds into a plant one time and forgot about it. But then four sprouts came up, and they grew bigger!" Intrigued by the random act, Wolf renamed his Minneapolis-based design and communications firm OrangeSeed Design.

To celebrate their first anniversary under their new namesake, the group at OrangeSeed Design thought it would be fun to host a party to reinforce their new identity and strengthen client and vendor relations. "We wanted to look within our existing client base and build those relationships really strong before we went out and brought in new clients," adds Wolf. With the idea of using orange trivia as a point of departure, the design team looked to the Internet for reference. With some choice facts selected, they adorned various promotional items, décor for the party, and a self-mailer invitation. "We put orange trees all over the office and set up fun little orange trivia signs all around. We even had orange drinks," shares Wolf. "We wanted the party to be fun and festive, to pull people back in."

The invitation presents an interesting piece of trivia, drawing the viewer to open the piece in search for an answer. The self-mailer opens via a side perforation. Inside is a gift—a collection of four orange trivia coasters held together by a plastic bag that is blindly adhered with staples. "The first challenge was coming up with the fold," says Wolf. "The coasters had to fit in tight enough in the middle of the piece so they didn't slide out." To get the construction just right, the design team produced several mockups. The piece had to hold the coasters securely, be machine folded, and fit within postal regulations under first-class dimensions. To bind the invitation, the firm wanted to try something a little different. Using a sewing machine, each mailer was stitched shut with Dual Duty brand thread in bright orange. To keep expenses to a minimum, the piece was digitally printed, the coasters piggybacked onto a client's print run, and everything hand-assembled in-house by the staff.

TECHNICAL TIPS

When the construction of your piece is critical, always do a prototype to scale and send a few pieces to yourself and your colleagues. This allows you to see how the piece handles during delivery and what it will potentially look like when it arrives at a client's office.

For a straight and consistent stitch, use a magnetic sewing machine guide. Each needle can stitch approximately twenty-five pieces before needing to be replaced. Dual Duty brand thread works best.

Orange cups filled with miniature orange trees surrounded the festive event. They served as a constant reminder of the company's new name, OrangeSeed Design.

As a party giveaway, customized labels adorned fresh oranges purchased at a local grocery store by the case. Oranges are also kept in a bowl in the studio at all times for clients, vendors, and other visitors. OrangeSeed Design is expecting their first harvest of oranges soon.

FIRM: ORANGESEED DESIGN

CREATIVE DIRECTOR: DAMIEN WOLF

DESIGNERS: DAMIEN WOLF, DALE MUSTFUL, JONATHAN HINZ, AND ADAM CARVER

PRINTING: DIGIT IMAGING (INVITATION) AND CHALLENGE PRINTING (COASTERS)

MANUFACTURER: ULINE (PLASTIC BAGS)

1

3

2

sweet impression

Each of the seven gum wrappers features a character expressing such emotions as *happiness*, *sadness*, and *anger*. A pack of five is wrapped in translucent paper and taped shut. The attention-getting collection is used to pique the interest of art buyers to the illustration style of Barbara Lipp.

The Graphic Artist Guild was having a trade show, and participating illustrator Barbara Lipp wanted to make a sweet impression with attendees. "Each artist had a table space for showing their portfolio. I'd never participated in this event before, but I assumed there would be plenty of promotional postcards being handed out," offers Lipp. "I was trying to think of something different and novel." Call it divine intervention or creative inspiration, but the idea of using gum just popped into the artist's head as a unique, portable, and delicious way of presenting her work. "The inherent silliness of using tiny gum wrappers to promote oneself appealed to me," Lipp adds. "It really came out of my desire to offer the people coming to the event something fun and different from all the other freebies." At the trade show, Lipp used the gum promotion to bring attention to her work, giving away approximately two hundred individual sticks to interested art directors and editors.

To produce the whimsical promotion, the artist went to the local grocery store and purchased gum in a variety of flavors. She opened the wrappers, measured and noted the dimensions, and started playing with various designs on the computer. She focused her attention on the faces of characters in her portfolio. Their engaging quality and ability to capture attention in a small-scale format made them the perfect subject matter for this promotion. To add a humorous twist and unify the images, the artist made up titles for each, using emotions like *happiness*, *anger*, and *sadness*. "I like the idea of creating gum that has these magical qualities if chewed," shares Lipp. "I thought I might even do a round of secondary emotions—ambivalent gum, envy gum, and manic gum." To create the finished look, Lipp simply repackaged the silver foil–enclosed gum with her newly designed wrappers, using glue stick as an adhesive. "The trickiest part was aligning the wrappers so that they folded around the edges in just the right place," admits Lipp. "I'd do it at night while watching television. It was like knitting!"

Because of the tremendous response at the guild event, Lipp decided to wrap the sticks into packs of five and mail them to editorial and book publishing art buyers along with a postcard and illustrated client list. "Art directors are absolutely bombarded with promotional mail," comments the artist. "But if they get a package and can feel that there is some little object inside, they will always check it out just from sheer curiosity. This doesn't guarantee you will get work, but it will get their attention." As the market for illustration narrows, the competition will intensify, leading, as Lipp feels, to "even more creative and bolder forms of promotion."

TECHNICAL TIPS

When you are reproducing text and images in a small format, it is important to keep them bold and simple for readability purposes. If you want to print the wrappers in-house, you can easily gang up eight wrapper designs to a sheet. To save money, everything can be trimmed and wrapped by hand. Retain the existing silver foil around the gum to avoid an additional process and expense.

The promotional pack is sent to prospective buyers with a client list and postcard. The illustrated client list serves as a way to show a variety of images from the artist's portfolio in an interesting way. The artist's logo and signature image, entitled the Angry Girl, appears on all of her promotional material as a unifying element.

Lipp has expanded her promotion work to include customized magnets. Each image is applied to self-adhesive business card–sized magnets that can be purchased in packages of fifty or one hundred. Each image is printed on glossy photo-quality paper. It is sent as a follow-up mailing, a reminder of the artist and her whimsical work.

1

3

FIRM: BARBARA LIPP ILLUSTRATION

CREATIVE DIRECTOR AND DESIGNER: BARBARA LIPP

ILLUSTRATION: BARBARA LIPP

MANUFACTURERS: OFFICEMAX (MAGNETS) AND VARIOUS BRANDS OF GUM

2

fresh start

"Real, raw and renovated" were the words that staff designer Shawn Murenbeeld used to describe the relocation of DWL's corporate headquarters from an old 800-square-foot (74-square-meter) piano factory to a newly renovated 3,700-square-foot (344-square-meter) space. The expansion marked a fresh start for the company, and what better than to document it with a special gift? "There was this whole new look," recalls Murenbeeld, "and I wanted something fun, unexpected, and memorable to raise the spirits of the staff."

With the fresh theme in mind, Murenbeeld came up with an interesting idea: T-shirts wrapped in meat trays like fresh produce in a supermarket. The designer chose to deliver the message on green cotton T-shirts, silk-screen-printed in red on both sides. The front of the shirt has a bold illustration of meat. On the back, various interpretations of the word *fresh* are outlined, symbolizing the renewed spirit that a fresh start in a new space brings. The sleeve of the shirt simply displays the company's identity. The printed T-shirts were folded and placed on white meat packing trays obtained at a local grocery store. To finish the look, each package was shrink-wrapped and labeled. "I wrapped 250 T-shirts with the butcher for two hours," says Murenbeeld. "He also gave me a whole roll of these labels that said 'ring in meat.' I couldn't refuse!"

The designer also created some labels of his own. "Every time I got meat at the store, I kept all the labels because I wanted to get a feel for the best features of each," notes Murenbeeld. "One thing I noticed about the labels was that they were so random. When the store printed them, no one thought carefully about the placement of the type." The designer tried to simulate that feel by overlapping the type in different areas. The custom label features expressions like *keep cool* and *fresh perspective*, a pseudo price listed as "$F.REE," the moving date masquerading as an expiration date, and a barcode to finish off the overall effect. Also noted is the firm's new address, conveniently positioned where a grocery store address might be found. To reveal the size of each shirt, small circular labels were printed and die-cut on fluorescent orange stock and applied to the outer package.

The T-shirt promotion was distributed to all DWL employees on the day the new office was complete. It was a big hit and enjoyed by all. "Actually, most of the people would not even open them," comments Murenbeeld. "Instead, they put the wrapped package on their wall and on their desk. People were asking for two—one to wear and one to keep. It made me happy."

TECHNICAL TIPS

Be as resourceful as you can be. Start with the best solution and never rule out potential sources, like the local supermarket butcher, who can help you realize your vision. To capture a sense of realism, always spend time researching. Sometimes the tiniest touches make the biggest impact.

1

Each cotton T-shirt is shrink-wrapped onto a Styrofoam tray and labeled, giving the effect of fresh produce in a supermarket. The custom label features various details that help make the package not only interesting but also functional. For instance, the moving date looks like an expiration date, while the firm's new address is positioned where a grocery store address might be found. A small circular fluorescent orange label cleverly reveals the size of the shirt.

2

The silk-screen-printed T-shirts are adorned with a bold and graphic illustration of meat. On the back, the definition of the word *fresh* is detailed to help communicate DWL's fresh start in a new space. The sleeve simply displays the company's name and logo.

1

2

FIRM: DWL INCORPORATED

CREATIVE DIRECTOR AND DESIGNER: SHAWN MURENBEELD

ILLUSTRATION: SHAWN MURENBEELD

PRINTING: THE BEANSTOCK GROUP

The poster features a graphic optical illusion on the back to complement the intriguing photography on the front. The illusionary effects make the piece not only different but also memorable. Each poster is rolled, sealed with a red sticker, and delivered to prospective buyers in a custom injection-molded tube.

To get prospective buyers to visit, bookmark, and license work from their Web site, Untitled knew they had to come up with a promotion that was a bit out of the ordinary so as to attract attention in the oversaturated stock photography market. Designer Zoe Scutts was pulled in to assist in the creation of an innovative, yet simple, promotional campaign. Taking inspiration from both the world of fine art and the medical industry, Untitled developed a unique presentation for their alternative and experimental work. "The poster was inspired by the abstract artist Bridget Reilly," notes photographer and founder Nick Veasey, "while the mailer was inspired by surgical swabs."

To make a lasting impression, the first mailing took the form of a keepsake. The device chosen to carry the message was a large, highly graphic poster displaying the work of several photographic artists in a unique and intriguing way. Further distinguishing the group, the poster was rolled, sealed, and shipped in a custom injection-molded tube made of 500-micron plastic. This not only provided an interesting presentation for the memorable Web site announcement but also protected the piece from the elements during delivery. "We tried to create something that the target audience would cherish," says Veasey.

A second, attention-getting promotion was sent as well. Round two packed its punch in a small, but effective, package. Sent in a medical swab pouch, the intimate accordion-folded brochure features the work of twelve photographers out of 106 currently represented in the contemporary image library at Untitled. Flexography, a process commonly used in the packaging industry, was employed to imprint the self-sealing bags. To stay within the limitations of this process, the graphics and text were kept simple and straightforward, directing the recipient to Untitled's stock site in a clear and unadorned fashion. Because of the number of folds in the fourteen-paneled piece, 80-gram Skyegloss was the thickest paper that fit within the packet's interior parameters.

With the entrance of large corporate stock houses into the photography business, the industry has seen an influx of mediocre and cliché images into the culture. This overabundant work, delivered at a discounted price, has created a wedge in the market, limiting commission work by building client loyalty through discounted stock sales. To control their destiny, photographers have united, creating alternative solutions for buyers. Taking matters into their own hands, they have created some of the best sources for innovative and creative stock photography available. "I had a few friends who were photographers, a collection of images, some money, and off we went," concludes Veasey. "Untitled is growing and getting better. The word is out, and some very good people are approaching us."

TECHNICAL TIPS

Because the space inside a swab packet is limited, use a thin stock for any promotional material you plan to fold up inside. When imprinting the packets, remember that you need to design within flexography's restrictions.

When custom designing with injection-molded plastic, give the manufacturer an accurate schematic drawing and a mock-up to work with. Always have a working model made to fully test your idea before you go into production.

2

Untitled's stock catalog is quite unique in that it profiles each photographer in his or her own specially designed section. Featured is the opening spread for photographer Nick Veasey's work.

A brochure, sent as a follow-up mailing in an adapted surgical swab pouch, features a range of images from the contemporary image library at Untitled. Two versions are available.

1

2

3

FIRMS: UNTITLED

CREATIVE DIRECTOR AND DESIGNER:

ZOE SCUTTS

PHOTOGRAPHY: UNTITLED.CO.UK

PRINTING: SPIN OFFSET (POSTER) AND

PRECISION COLOUR PRINTING (BROCHURE)

BINDERY: SPEMA

MANUFACTURERS: MACPAC (INJECTION-MOLDED TUBE)

AND RIVERSIDE MEDICAL PACKAGING

COMPANY LIMITED (SELF-SEALING POLYETHYLENE BAGS)

alternative uses and add-ons

chapter four: **ALTERNATIVE USES**

Designers are reusing existing elements in a variety of ways to complement their promotions. Film canisters, wallet holders, and dog tags are finding secondary functions and miniature spoons, seeds, and customized sound chips are being added as accents—the finishing touch that makes a promotion memorable. Often, the most minute of details can make the biggest impact. "We put a premium on resourcefulness and are always on the lookout for mechanical processes or techniques that can be repurposed and reapplied to create more interest, personality, or a unique character," shares Ron Miriello of Miriello Grafico. "During our travels, we've collected a hand-lettering perforation machine from Milan, a page-numbering stamp from Japan, and a 1930s postage stamp perforator from an antique dealer in Orange County, California. We've also got a small, sewing-machine-size letterpress printer from the 1920s. The tools are a symbol of our interest and respect for personal communications in a time of mass production. When mixed with modern imagery and technique, they can create an interesting tension."

When you choose to supplement your work with add-ons or want to reuse elements in a different way, make sure they enhance your concept in some way. Using something just for the sake of being different is a waste of time and money that only results in a confusing overall message. "The primary impetus for alternative uses and add-ons should always be an effort to improve the effectiveness of a design," offers Marcie Carson of IE Design. "It should unify and complete the design, not clutter it." Never stop asking yourself how you can improve on something you have created. Questioning your efforts will challenge you to strive for excellence each time. When creatives push the envelope and try new things, the industry will evolve and grow as a result.

"I wanted to create a promotion that would identify me as an idea person, someone who can come up with interesting concepts and put things together in a kind of unusual way," says designer and illustrator Charlotte Noruzi. "To get art directors and editors to look at my work, I wanted something that was not only fun but also memorable." Targeted toward the publishing industry, Noruzi developed a series of four direct-mail promotions based on well-known trade book titles. "I did a fictional correspondence between characters from books I thought people would know of and that would be interesting and diverse enough to do a self-promotion with," she adds. *Faust*, *Bridget Jones's Diary*, and *A Handful of Dust* were all illustrated and cleverly presented as postage stamps alongside handwritten envelopes and personalized letters. In each mailing, the reader is a voyeur into the lives of several main characters in the respective books.

The elongated shape of the stamps helped maintain the vertical book cover format, while the hand-lettering and graphics brought interest and intrigue to each mailing. The postage rate, replaced by a telephone number, was the only point of contact. Noruzi enhanced each mailing with prominent storyline elements such as cigarettes, matches, burn marks, dripped wax, and small pieces of cut paper. "Bridget Jones, in her letter to Mark Darcy, gives away her last cigarette in an attempt to stop her vices," shares Noruzi. "There is no return address on the letter to Miss Brenda Last because the writer, Tony Last, was off on a safari in the jungle and had no address." On the back of each envelope, small details were extracted from the selected book covers to maintain visual harmony throughout. Such finishing touches show the illustrator's attention to detail and keen ability to convey key points within each story.

The entire promotional series was printed using a color laser printer. The die-cut details were created by hand with perforated scissors. Each stamp was adhered with glue stick to the appropriate envelope with great precision. If a stamp was not positioned just right, it would not accurately line up with its corresponding cancellation mark, the date each mailing was sent. The complete promotional ensemble was hand-assembled by the artist. "I think it is worth the investment to spend a little bit more time and money on your promotion to create something that will really stand out," remarks Noruzi. The three fictional correspondences were mailed at two-week intervals. A final mailing, showing other examples of the artist's work, served as a follow-up. Only twenty-five pieces were created.

TECHNICAL TIPS

A relatively inexpensive handmade promotion that has a strong idea behind it will always champion over even the most highly expensive ones, where the concept was never really considered. Add-ons such as custom-designed stamps, matches, and cigarettes can be quite engaging, encouraging the reader to be a part of the story.

With the purchase of perforated scissors, a nice decorative edge can be created. The application of things such as cut paper, dripped wax, and splattered ink are all quite easy to do and can add interesting effects to the paper surface. If you choose to add a burned effect to your promotion, do it after the sheet has already been imprinted. Also have lots of extras available, as the process is not so forgiving.

The book, *Bridget Jones's Diary*, deals with the main character's quest to stop her addictions. A cigarette is enclosed to Mark Darcy, another character in the book, as a gesture of Bridget's attempt to quit. The whimsical hand-lettering, graphics, and copy bring out the main character's personality. They also show the artist's ability to conceptualize, design, and, of course, illustrate. This is the first in the series of mailings.

1

FIRM: QUESTION DESIGN

CREATIVE DIRECTOR AND DESIGNER:

CHARLOTTE NORUZI

ILLUSTRATION: CHARLOTTE NORUZI

MANUFACTURERS: KATE'S PAPERIE

(WAX, STATIONERY PAPER, AND ENVELOPES)

AND JAM PAPER (ENVELOPES)

fictional correspondence

continued

A Handful of Dust is accented by little cut pieces of paper that are adhered to the inside flap of the envelope. The tiny black scraps are symbolic of what the life of Tony Last has become, a handful of dust. The letterhead features Victorian graphics taken from a Dover book. This is the second mailing in the promotional series.

2

Faust, the third mailing, shows Noruzi's ability to illustrate a very different kind of story, one more dramatic in nature. To create the burn marks, the artist used both a lighter and a match held at varying distances from the envelope. The back of the envelope is accented and sealed with colored wax, which was heated and allowed to drip on.

Designed like a set of stamps, the final promotion ties the previous mailings together and serves as a follow-up device. Each stamp shows a different book cover design, demonstrating the breadth and diversity of the artist's repertoire of work. The follow-up promotion is sent in a white envelope with a perforated label that nicely ties in with the overall stamp concept.

3

4

techno dog

A mechanical wind-up toy transforms into a techno dog, announcing the *Bark's* newly developed Web site. The industrial-looking canine is distributed in a silver antistatic bag punched with holes to facilitate "breathing." The label, economically printed in-house with an Epson 1520 inkjet printer on high-quality, non adhesive paper, is applied with a spray adhesive to seal the package shut. It also provides operating instructions for the recipient's new pet. The launch and shipping date is stamped in red ink as an accent. The promotion is shipped in a cardboard box custom-wrapped in yellow.

The *Bark*, a San Francisco–based literary arts quarterly for dog lovers, wanted to announce the unleashing of their newly designed Web site to top advertisers, distributors, and investors of the magazine. Red Canoe, developers of the site, wanted to do something a bit different to capture the attention of their client's target audience. "We had just completed two sites. The first one was an investor demo, which was successful enough to lead to a complete site redesign and development," recalls cofounder Deb Koch. "The *Bark's* publisher and editor knew that promoting the Web site would be crucial."

To bridge the gap between the tactile and the online worlds, the design team at Red Canoe started looking through their vast resources in search of the perfect vehicle to carry their message. After discovering this real eclectic wind-up toy with an uncanny resemblance to a dog, the design team had the starting point they were looking for. From there, a bone-shaped dog tag, engraved with the Web site's address (www.thebark.com), just seemed like a natural add-on for the techno pet to wear. "As would any useful dog tag, it provided the doggie's home address information, which in this case was a play on words, given the Internet meaning of *home*," adds Koch. "In the instructions, we suggested that once the little guy was on the move, one might follow him to his new home and, to do that, one had to read the dog tag."

The wind-up dog arrives packaged in a silver antistatic bag complete with air holes for the little metallic creature to breathe through during its journey through the mail. "The nostalgic memories many people have of bringing home a pet in a box and poking breathing holes in it was an experience and a feeling we hoped to be able to bag," explains Koch. A bright yellow custom-designed label provided not only shipping information but also operating instructions for the small mechanical canine. As an additional finishing detail, the shipping date, which announced the launch day of the newly developed site, was imprinted on the labels with a rubber stamp. "All of the wording on the label was reduced to the bare minimum to express a manufacturing and industrial trompe l'oeil," details Koch. "For us, the 'less is more' philosophy is expressed in the details."

The promotion was successful for both the *Bark* and Red Canoe. "In addition to achieving specific advertising goals for the client, the piece also drew attention to our Web site design and development work as well as our identity, branding, and promotional capabilities," Koch concludes.

TECHNICAL TIPS

When utilizing vendors outside the communications market, don't assume they will completely understand your out-of-the-ordinary requests. Be patient, keep in constant communication, and put all of your correspondence in writing so everything is completely clear. To get text imprinted on a dog tag, make sure the wholesale supply house understands that what is to be imprinted has to be exactly the way you have designed it. They have a tendency to change the font size and drop to two lines where they see fit. For punching holes in antistatic bags, a conventional hand-held single-hole puncher works the best. Last, always request samples and plan enough time to do things right, thinking ahead at every step.

3

The doglike toy winds up and encourages the recipient to follow it home. The bone-shaped collar around its neck makes the connection between the canine's home and the Web site home page.

A full-page, four-color print ad was created in addition to the direct mail promotional announcement.

The *Bark*'s Web site, www.thebark.com, and the announcement feature similar design elements to make the transition from print to online a familiar one.

CLIENT: THE BARK

FIRM: RED CANOE

CREATIVE DIRECTOR: DEB KOCH

DESIGNER: CAROLINE KAVANAGH

PRINTING: EPSON 1520 INKJET PRINTER (WRAPPING PAPER AND LABELS)

SPECIAL TECHNIQUES: R. C. STEELE (ENGRAVING)

MANUFACTURERS: KIKKERLAND DESIGN, INC. (WIND-UP DOG),
R. C. STEELE (DOG TAGS) AND ULINE (ANTISTATIC BAGS AND SHIPPING BOXES)

1

2

4

mini-catalog

Empty film canisters, obtained at a local photo lab, contain minicatalogs featuring the work of photographer Luka Mjeda. Each catalog is offset-printed, hand-cut, and laminated to simulate the look and feel of film. Once inserted and rolled, the catalog is placed in a plastic container.

The impetus for this minicatalog began as an assignment from Igor Zidić, the director of the Modern Gallery in Croatia. Luka Mjeda was hired to photograph several Croatian artists who were to participate in a traveling exhibition. Excited about the resulting work, Mjeda was eager to find a way to package it in a presentation that was as engaging as the photography. The biggest challenge was figuring out how to create an interesting promotional piece that was also lightweight and easily portable. Mjeda and designer Danijel Popović worked together to develop an innovative solution—a minicatalog rolled up inside a used film canister. "I have always had problems explaining to people what I do and why I want to photograph them, and it is difficult to carry my big book around," notes Mjeda. "This catalog is like my business card, and I always have it with me. It's an icebreaker." The fine- and commercial-art photographer always likes to deliver the compact promotion by hand, as he is interested in recipients' reactions to the piece.

Two versions of the promotion were created, one in English and the other in Croatian. Each version was printed on Sappi Magnomat (115 gr/m²) stock that was later sealed in plastic to simulate a filmlike surface and to protect the piece from tears and scratches. Each printed catalog was hand-inserted into an empty film canister by permanently adhering the piece to the core with clear tape. Once the catalog was attached, it was simply rolled back up, leaving out just enough to give the appearance of the beginning of a film roll. To save money, each catalog was hand-cut and inserted into the canisters by Mjeda. The empty canisters and plastic containers were collected from local photo labs. Mjeda assembled a total of 1,200 promotions.

Referred to by Mjeda as the "canned catalog," the minipromotion features twenty-three Croatian artists, from painters and sculptors to installation and video artists. The slice-of-life portraits reveal the artists' inspirations, their work, and their surroundings. "Looking at them in their studios, you can get an idea about what kind of an artist they are," adds Mjeda. Copies of the catalog reside in the permanent collection of Kodak and the Victoria and Albert Museum in London. A book entitled *Luka Mjeda: Croatian Artists*, published by The Modern Gallery, nicely complements the promotion. The portraits were so captivating that Mjeda himself was included in the traveling exhibition that journeyed through Chile, Brazil, Argentina, and Bolivia.

TECHNICAL TIPS

If you choose to trim the work by hand, you must cut each laminated press sheet one at a time. Because the plastic sheets tended to shift, cutting multiple pieces at once would create a lot of waste. Adhering and inserting a catalog into a film canister takes about two minutes.

The lightweight and thought-provoking promotion captures the world of twenty-three of Croatia's best artists in a variety of disciplines.

A full list of credits regarding the exhibition is on the back of the promotion.

2

FIRM: S.L.M. D.O.O.

CREATIVE DIRECTORS:

DANIJEL POPOVIĆ AND LUKA MJEDA

DESIGNER: DANIJEL POPOVIĆ

PHOTOGRAPHY: LUKA MJEDA

PRINTER: AKD

MANUFACTURERS: KODAK, FUJI, AND AGFA

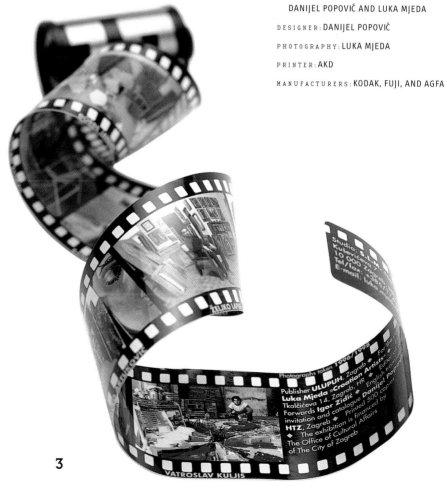

1

3

meet
the family

Designed to simulate a collection of snap-shots, the series of personalized business cards presents the staff of BBK Studio in a fun and creative way. The piece can remain inside the tin container or hang on a wall. The promotion is distributed in a white corrugated box stuffed with orange crinkle wrap and sealed with the firm's mailing label.

Excited about their new office space, BBK Studio plunged into redesigning their entire business system. To celebrate, the design firm wanted to host a party for clients and vendors alike. But as time went on, the busy studio got sidetracked with other work. Soon, too much time had passed, and a party was no longer appropriate. "We had grown quite a bit, and our clients didn't know about the new people we had hired either," adds creative director and designer Yang Kim. Wanting to salvage their initial idea of an open house, the firm came up with an interesting alternative. "We decided we would do a studio tour, but in an analog fashion," explains Kim.

Because the design firm's new visual identity contained quite a unique collection of business cards, Kim thought that she could use this somehow. "The cards in themselves are almost like miniresumes, listing everyone's different personality and interests," she notes. "I was thinking that the cards, in a way, were a little collection of personal snapshots. It was almost like the proud father who pulls out photos of his family." With that idea in mind, the design firm searched for vendors to create a wallet-style plastic sleeve that could house standard-size business cards. After looking through several options in an array of plastics, the designer chose a custom plastic sleeve that was accordion-folded with a small tab at the top, allowing it to be hung if desired. "I thought it would be useful to be able to put the piece up on a tackboard to reference several people at a glance," remarks Kim. The cards were printed on the front with two PMS colors, metallic silver and bright orange. The backs of the cards were dou-ble-hit with the orange for solid coverage. To accent the BBK Studio logo, a clear thermography was applied. The entire piece was coated with an overall aqueous varnish to protect the orange ink from rubbing off the uncoated stock.

A silver tin with rounded corners was chosen to house the pullout promotion. "Because our system was designed using silver and orange, it made sense to use something metallic," acknowledges Kim. "Also, if you decided to take the piece out and hang it, you could reuse the tin for something else." The piece was sent in a white corrugated box stuffed with orange crinkle wrap and sealed with a mailing label. With a little ingenuity, BBK Studio was able to successfully introduce their new look, space, and staff through an upbeat and entertaining promotion.

TECHNICAL TIPS

Certain colors, because of their chemical makeup, dry more slowly than others. If you are looking to double-hit a color, especially on uncoated stock, talk to your printer about potential drying problems. An overall varnish may have to be applied to protect the slow-drying color from later rubbing off.

The business cards provide insight into the various personalities at BBK Studio. They are printed in the firm's corporate colors, bright orange and silver. The backs are double-hit with orange, and clear thermography is applied to call attention to the logo. An over-all aqueous varnish is applied to both sides.

The new business system—pocket folder, notecard, various labels, letterhead, envelope, and business card—reflects the energy and enthusiasm of this growing firm. The rounded corners and circular accents throughout play nicely off the dot pattern used in the BBK Studio logo.

FIRM: BBK STUDIO

CREATIVE DIRECTOR AND DESIGNER:
    YANG KIM

PRINTING: FOREMOST GRAPHICS

MANUFACTURER: RG CREATIONS

1

2

3

do it
to music!

The mission of Brown & Company Design was to put together a promotion that really communicated how they worked and who they were as a company—fun, energetic, and a bit eclectic. They also wanted to shake things up creatively in the studio, encouraging each other to work outside their comfort zone. In search for a distinctive vehicle to communicate their message, the firm decided to really push the envelope and put their process to music! Because many staff members are musically inclined, the instrumental compositions were a breeze. The real challenge for many was overcoming the fear of performing in a studio, standing alone with headphones on in front of a microphone and singing. "When we handed out the assignments, some people volunteered right up front and others had to be coerced a bit," recalls designer and musician Chris Lamy.

The project was given a set budget, and everyone was assigned a stage of the firm's working process to write lyrics about, a genre of music to be inspired by, and some music to sing to. "We took our process and identified recognizable milestones, from the sales pitch to the delivery," adds Lamy. Every album cover was thoroughly researched so the design accurately represented the colors, typefaces, and imagery indicative of each style of music being portrayed. Each assignment was critiqued by the entire group, giving the overall project a cohesive look and creating a sense of ownership by all.

The first step was to record the music on tape. "The musicians and vocalists performed their tracks, and they were mixed together. Once we were happy with it, the tracks were mixed down from twenty-four tracks to two tracks (stereo) and burned onto a mixed disc," explains Lamy. The next step was to get a premaster made. "DeCato Sound made each individual track the same volume, inserted even spaces between songs, edited the noise, and put the songs in order," continues Lamy. "Upon approval, the premaster was delivered to Crooked Cove for the CD plant, US Optical Disc, to replicate. Crooked Cove coordinated and handled all of the paperwork, legalities, and actual ordering of the CDs." Normally, CDs are put in jewel cases and shrink-wrapped. To save money, the design firm hand-collated and stuffed the CDs in their own sleeves.

By exploring venues of creativity outside their area of expertise, the staff at Brown & Company was able to put together an attention-getting promotion that has not only invigorated the entire group but also gotten them national exposure far surpassing their expectations. "New Hampshire Public Radio had us down at their studios for a show just on the CD. The show was so popular that they reran it during a pledge drive, and it was one of their most successful half hours," exclaims Lamy. "When it all came together, there were sparks flying around here, and everyone was very proud. It really challenged us creatively and paid off in the end." Mission accomplished!

TECHNICAL TIPS

Creating a promotion such as this is no small feat. Many details must be attended to in order for the project to succeed. Time must be scheduled for design, musical composition, writing, rehearsing, and coordinating with all of the various vendors, from the recording studio to the final printing and replication house. In addition, a lot of administrative work must be done to ensure no one else owns the music. Once the music is deemed original, it must be copyrighted to protect it and the label art. (Crooked Cove handled these administrative details in this case). To organize such an endeavor, it is best to treat yourself like a client and follow the protocol that has already made you successful. Set a budget and timeline, and divide the workload among teams.

1

Each Kraft CD sleeve, purchased in bulk in a standard design, is hand-printed on the front, inside, and spine with custom-made rubber stamps. The enclosed CD is professionally recorded, mastered, replicated, and printed. Each package is individually shrink-wrapped and delivered to prospective and existing clientele as a self-mailer.

2

To communicate to clients who they were and how they worked, Brown & Company Design set their process to music. Each insert, representing a different stage of their working process, is designed to look like an album cover. Each depicting a different decade and style of music, the covers cleverly evoke the personality of this innovative and eclectic firm.

1

2

FIRM: BROWN & COMPANY DESIGN

CREATIVE DIRECTOR: DAVID MARKOVSKY

DESIGNERS: CHRIS LAMY, MARY JO BROWN, CHRIS HAMER, SCOTT BUCHANAN, JODI HOLT, ANDREA ADAMS, MATT TALBOT, D.J. BURDETTE, CLAUDIA KAERNER, DAVID MARKOVSKY, AND TRICIA MILLER

ILLUSTRATION: ERIC ANDREWS, SCOTT BUCHANAN, AND MATT TALBOT

PHOTOGRAPHY: DAVID GOODMAN, CLAUDIA KAERNER, AND TRICIA MILLER

MUSIC COMPOSERS: CHRIS LAMY AND MATT TALBOT

LYRICISTS AND VOCALS: BROWN & COMPANY STAFF

INSTRUMENTS: CHRIS LAMY (GUITAR), MATT TALBOT (BASS GUITAR, BANJO, AND ACCORDION), DAVID MORRIS (PERCUSSION AND PAN FLUTE), BILL RIENDUEA (ACCORDION), MARY JO BROWN (PIANO), ERIK EVENSEN (SAXOPHONE), AND ALICEN BROWN (BARITONE GUITAR)

EFFECTS: DAVID MORRIS, JODI HOLD, AND CLAUDIA KAERNER

PRINTING: RAM PRINTING (INSERT COVERS)

SPECIAL TECHNIQUES: THE ELECTRIC CAVE (RECORDING STUDIO), DECATO SOUND (CD MASTERING), CROOKED COVE (DISC PRINTING AND REPLICATION COORDINATION), AND US OPTICAL DISC (CD REPLICATION AND GLASS MASTERING)

MANUFACTURERS: CALUMET CONTAINER (CD SLEEVES) AND BOB'S RUBBER STAMPS (RUBBER STAMP)

LISTEN TO THE CD: WWW.BROWNTONE.COM

that finishing touch!

"Good Gracious! came into our offices with a folder they had been using—a standard two-pocket piece that was overflowing with clippings, press releases, recipes, and a cover letter," recalls creative director and designer Marcie Carson. "It was not an effective introduction." To get the events company off to a better start, the designer immediately knew she had to create a piece that would not only conceal much of the extraneous paperwork but also make a more memorable first impression overall. "Good Gracious! creates amazing events and focuses on every detail, from the impeccable menu to the imaginative environment surrounding it," says Carson. "We wanted this piece to feel much like the events—captivating, delicious, organized, whimsical, and always, always creative." The target market for the promotion ranged from planners of large corporate functions to intimate birthday parties.

With a clear direction in mind, the designer put pencil to paper and laid out her idea. "I immediately had a vision for this piece. I saw the finished folder in my head before I even sat down at my desk," says Carson. "We did present one other comp to give the client an option, but I knew that this would be the one." The result was a stunning custom die-cut pocket folder that incorporated the company's existing corporate colors and logo mark. "Good Gracious! did not have a brand identity when they approached us. They did have an existing logo that was quite nice, but felt a bit like fast food," the designer admits. "Because they did have some equity in this logo, I felt strongly about utilizing the existing mark as is. In the end, we were able to tie it in nicely, giving it a more elegant place in which to live."

To add richness to the outside of the folder, a double hit of royal purple was applied. A bright red, yellow, and purple sticker sealed the self-mailing package, creating curiosity about what may unfold. Once the seal is broken, the inside reveals a miniature spoon cleverly inserted into yet another enclosure, enticing the viewer to continue to explore. "I am frequently challenging our design team by saying 'That's great, but how can we make it better?'" offers Carson. "On this project, I asked myself that very question, and Good Gracious! ended up with a playful golden spoon—an appropriate addition, as the letterhead design contained a photo of a fork and knife." Underneath, a business card and stationery provide both contact information and a nicely designed environment for support materials. The ethereal and dreamlike montage interior evokes the ambience, elegance, and sophistication that a Good Gracious! event provides. Overall, the promotion is a beautiful blend of both form and function.

TECHNICAL TIPS

When you have a self-mailer that needs to make a memorable impression, always do a test mailing so potential problems can be ironed out in advance. To keep growing as a designer, never stop asking yourself how you can improve on something that you have created. Questioning your efforts will challenge you to strive for excellence each time. Often, the minutest details make the biggest impact.

The stunning jewel-toned package is accented by the company's logo, which was applied as a seal. Inside the self-mailer is another enclosure of sorts. A small golden spoon add-on piques curiosity and encourages the viewer to explore further. For durability and protection during delivery, the piece is printed with an overall varnish on 100-lb. Fox River Starwhite Vicksburg cover.

The curvilinear die-cut folder is not only attractive but also highly functional. Inside, a business card and custom-designed stationery provide contact and support information, organizing and adding elegance to the overflow of materials that once cluttered the event company's previous collateral. The piece was both mailed and given out by hand.

CLIENT: GOOD GRACIOUS! EVENTS

FIRM: [I]E DESIGN

CREATIVE DIRECTOR AND DESIGNER: MARCIE CARSON

PHOTOGRAPHY: STOCK

PRINTING: SOUTHERN CALIFORNIA GRAPHICS

BINDERY: CUSTOM DISPLAY

SPECIAL TECHNIQUES: CUSTOM DISPLAY (DIE-CUTTING)

MANUFACTURER: CREATIVE BEGINNINGS (SPOON)

Motive Design Research LLC, Wordslinger, and Robert Horsley Printing decided to combine their efforts, producing a New Year's promotion as a way to connect and build relationships with clients, valued suppliers, friends, and colleagues. In these uncertain times, the collaborative group thought it was important to shed light on the newfound possibilities that each year brings. "Over the past five years, we have developed a reputation for interesting, giftlike holiday promotions," acknowledges creative director Michael Connors. "But we, like many other people, were in a more somber mood this year and felt we should do something more meaningful."

With Planting a New Year as their concept, the design team began researching books and the Internet, inundating themselves with the practice of gardening. "In a brainstorming meeting, we came up with the idea of using seeds because they represent change, growth, and new beginnings, many of the same things a new year represents," adds Connors. "Adhering them to the cover immediately piqued the interest of recipients, and it was also a good way to incorporate individual greetings from each company." The seeds chosen were a western wildflower mix that requires minimal maintenance—a wise choice for the busy professionals who were to receive the package. "We decided that any one kind of flower—forget-me-nots, for example—would have limited the message to something too specific," Connors acknowledges. "We felt the wildflower mix was not only the easiest to use but was also in keeping with the spirit of the design." The seeds and insert card were packaged inside a small glassine envelope and adhered to the cover by a custom-made label. Throughout the saddle-stitched booklet, subtle relationships are drawn between gardening and the growing of one's future, business and personal. "The parallels between a garden and a life are unavoidable, and there's no time like a new year to make us aware of the connections. You can always do better and you can always do worse," shares collaborator Brittany Stromberg. "Each new year and each garden is what it is, yet they tell us everything about the people who plan, plant, and tend to them."

The greeting of good tidings has yielded new business for the collaborative team. "People we haven't talked to in ages have called and e-mailed to say how happy they were to receive it and that they couldn't wait to scatter the seeds," says Connors. "One former client of ours called and set up a meeting to discuss new possibilities of working together." Only 450 pieces were produced and divided among the collaborators.

TECHNICAL TIPS

When sending seeds, choose plants that are easy to maintain and can grow in the climate of the target audience. If you are shipping internationally, check with Customs for pertinent regulations. When packing seeds make sure the envelope or container is tightly sealed, as seeds are tiny and find their way through the smallest of holes.

The saddle-stitched promotion commences with the presentation of seeds, a beautiful mix of low-maintenance wildflowers. Along with the seeds, a customized card is included, individualizing the package for each company. Both are housed in a glassine envelope and adhered to the cover with a custom-made label. Each booklet is placed in a drawstring bag and distributed to clients, prospects, suppliers, friends, and colleagues.

The little book takes the reader through the entire process of gardening, starting with good compost, sowing seeds, watering, maintenance, and, of course, watching the wildflowers grow and change. The layout is a nice mix of utilitarianism and elegance.

2

ideas are

seeds.

1

FIRMS: MOTIVE DESIGN RESEARCH LLC, WORDSLINGER, AND ROBERT HORSLEY PRINTING

CREATIVE DIRECTORS: MICHAEL CONNORS AND KARI STRAND

DESIGNER: PETER AUGUST ANDERSON

ILLUSTRATION: PETER AUGUST ANDERSON

PHOTOGRAPHY: TOM CONNORS

COPYWRITING: BRITTANY STROMBERG

PRINTING: ROBERT HORSLEY PRINTING

BINDERY: SEATTLE BINDERY

MANUFACTURERS: ULINE (DRAWSTRING BAG), WILDSEED FARMS (SEEDS), AND PAPER MART (GLASSINE ENVELOPE)

To connect with clients, prospects, and friends, the creative team at Miriello Grafico wanted to make a year-end promotion that would touch people. "We were looking for something to symbolize the close of a difficult and challenging year for most everyone," remarks creative director Ron Miriello. "The idea of soap as a new, clean start fit with our search for a handmade and personal item that people would value."

To make the piece special, the creative team worked with a skin- and body-products specialist to design and develop an original blend of soap. After testing several recipes, a combination of such natural ingredients as oatmeal, lavender, coconut, and essential oils made for a soothing and sensual bath bar. "When asked what we wanted to be channeled into the soap, we said extra peace and prosperity," recalls Miriello. To further personalize the soap, the design team explored various shapes and signature engravings. However, when manufacturing limitations confined the soap to a traditional rectangular shape, they began to examine packaging alternatives to make their mark.

Because of the soap's unrefined texture, the team went in search of natural materials that conveyed a handmade and unfinished quality. A Kraft box with metal closures, available standard, was the perfect vehicle. To accent the surface, a customized mailing label and adhesive seal were added. Inside the box, a muslin drawstring bag imprinted with rubber stamps provided yet another layer of packaging, further piquing the recipient's curiosity. To give the promotion an artistic flair, each bag was individually numbered with a signature impression made using an automatic counter, traditionally used by manuscript editors to number document pages. "We liked the unique numbering system so much that we decided to apply it to the outside label on the box as well," adds designer Dennis Garcia. To deliver the message of a fresh and clean new year, a customized hang tag was attached to the drawstring of each muslin bag. The tag also served as a place to list the ingredients used in the making of this premium-blend bath bar. To lock in its sweet aroma, each bar was shrink-wrapped with a custom die-cut label adhered on top, adding just the right amount of decoration to the natural surface.

For the design firm, the intimate and personal gift was a huge success, reinforcing their reputation for being innovators. "We're still getting requests and handing out select samples to new prospects over a year later," concludes Miriello.

TECHNICAL TIPS

When packaging handmade soap, be aware that the natural oils may stick and leave a slight residue on most paper surfaces that it comes in contact with. Glassine paper and plastic seem to provide the best nonstick and stain-resistant options.

1

The giftlike promotion is concealed in a muslin drawstring bag whose raw texture and natural coloring add to the handmade and tactile quality of the overall piece. Custom-made rubber stamps are used to imprint the surface. In addition, each piece is individually numbered with an automatic counter, giving it the feel of a signature limited edition. To deliver the message of a fresh start for the new year, a custom-printed label is adhered to a hang tag and fastened to the drawstring bag. To complete the package, the promotion is placed inside a Kraft box and filled with packing tinsel. A decorative mailing label wraps the box, and an adhesive strip provides additional sealing support.

2

The handmade soap, a premium blend of essential oils and natural ingredients, is shrink-wrapped and decorated with a custom die-cut label. Its organic properties are said to bring peace and prosperity to those who use it.

1

2

FIRM: MIRIELLO GRAFICO

CREATIVE DIRECTORS:

RON MIRIELLO AND MARK MURPHY

DESIGNER: DENNIS GARCIA

ILLUSTRATION: DENNIS GARCIA

PRINTING: NEYENESCH PRINTERS INC.

SPECIAL TECHNIQUES:

NEYENESCH PRINTERS INC. (SHRINK-WRAPPING)

MANUFACTURERS: PEGGY RICHARDS (HANDMADE SOAP),

MASON BOX COMPANY (BOX AND PACKING TINSEL),

SAN FRANCISCO HERB COMPANY (DRAW STRING MUSLIN BAG),

CALIFORNIA STAMP COMPANY (CUSTOM STAMP),

AND GYPSY OFFICE SUPPLY COMPANY (HANG TAGS)

brand
survival

The brand-survival package contains an instructional manual, emergency rations, inspirational imagery, a pocketknife, and a flashlight. It is distributed in a silver pouch that is heat sealed and labeled. The color scheme, text, and icons are all inspired by safety graphics. Only 150 were produced. They were either hand-delivered or mailed to both existing and prospective clientele.

"To survive in the business world today, with the brand-conscious consumer, it is essential to have in place a well-designed identity implemented effectively and consistently," says creative director and designer Alexander Lloyd. "To that end, we wanted to show how our company could help businesses achieve this." To create an awareness of the importance and value of branding, Lloyd's Graphic Design and Communication put together a survival kit of sorts. The idea plays up on the need for companies to survive in a marketplace that is stagnant and starving for distinction. To make the package fun and memorable, a humorous twist was introduced. "As in many of my promos, I use a lot of tongue-in-cheek humor, playing the theme to its extreme," admits Lloyd. "In this case, I refer to how many business corporate identities are in such a bad state that they are really in need of emergency repair and should immediately consult a design professional qualified in brand aid, brand resuscitation, and corporate identity crisis management." Lloyd's Graphic Design and Communication to the rescue!

The brand survival kit contains the all-important spiral-bound manual, which begins by sharing insightful information on the need for companies to build brand recognition. It closes by showcasing the design firm's strong brand development capabilities through a diverse array of identity work. To push the playful concept a bit further, a pocketknife, flashlight, and emergency rations are included as the appropriate essentials for surviving the jungle of today's volatile marketplace. Each of the add-ons was sourced from a local retailer. The outer sleeves of the brain- and brand-stimulating candy bars were removed, and custom self-adhesive labels were applied. As stated on the back of the bar, "It will put you in the right frame of mind to tackle any brand design or redesign traumas you may face." Lloyd observes, "The strong yellow- and black-text-oriented graphics have a practical, no-nonsense, utilitarian feel that reflect the nature of safety information and official survival literature." To shed a light of hope for the truly brand-impaired, a CD-ROM of inspirational imagery was also included.

The promotion was delivered in a heat-sealed, reflective silver pouch reminiscent of a survival blanket. A custom-designed label and a small note enclosed the silver package, reminding recipients of the blessings a new year brings. The promotion was distributed to both existing and prospective clientele in need of immediate brand assistance or resuscitation. Let's hope they survive!

TECHNICAL TIPS

Think of the promotions you put out as an extension of your personality. It is just as important to reveal something about yourself and what it might be like to work with you, as it is to show what you are capable of. When you seek clients, you are also developing relationships.

Each French-folded page of *The Ultimate Brand Survival Manual* juxtaposes insightful text with visually compelling imagery to deliver the brand-building message. In the back, the spiral-bound manual showcases Lloyd's Graphic Design and Communication's portfolio of brand development work. It comes wrapped by a bellyband with an inspirational CD-ROM.

A chocolate bar, a flashlight, and a utility pocketknife all serve as concept-enhancing add-ons to the brand survival package.

1

2

FIRM: LLOYD'S GRAPHIC DESIGN & COMMUNICATION

CREATIVE DIRECTOR AND DESIGNER:
ALEXANDER LLOYD

ILLUSTRATION: ALEXANDER LLOYD

PHOTOGRAPHY: ALEXANDER LLOYD

PRINTING: BLENHEIM PRINTING CO.
AND BOS PRINT (ADHESIVE LABELS)

BINDERY: BLENHEIM PRINTING CO. (COPPER SPIRAL BINDING)

MANUFACTURERS: CAS-PAK PRODUCTS LTD. (FOIL POUCHES)
AND LOCAL RETAILER (FLASHLIGHT, POCKETKNIFE, AND JEWEL CASES)

3

To survive in today's volatile marketplace, creatives are adopting an entrepreneurial mindset and exploring venues outside the traditional nomenclature. "The industry is in flux, and you have to work harder to get that client to spend money," says Harvey Hirsch of Media Consultants. "Companies that did business for years one way are now learning that they must do business another way if they are to survive." Charlotte Noruzi of Question Design agrees. "We need to step outside of the usual markets and research other viable directions. The business stays alive and vital by taking risks and exploring new avenues."

To ride the wave of instability in the marketplace, many creatives are diversifying into other areas and, essentially, becoming their own client. "Our firm decided to venture into retail, a new line of business for us, primarily to gain greater control over our own financial future," admits Pam Williams of Williams and House. "In the field of design and communications, the work we do is dictated by what our clients need at a given time. If a client decides to cut a budget, that might mean cutting a project or two that we were really counting on. We needed to take on greater control of our destiny and revenue stream." By utilizing their visual communications expertise, the partners at Williams and House were able to launch their own line of merchandise and apparel. "This experience can only enhance our current business," adds Williams. "It's one thing to talk the talk with clients. But it's an entirely different thing to be able to say you've walked the walk yourself."

Another direction that many are taking is venturing into partnerships with clients. "We did a joint venture with a shampoo company," offers Ric Riordon of the Riordon Design Group, Inc. "We shared the risk, doing the creative for a new brand. They made it and we promoted it. That partnership allowed us to be very free with our ideas. With our investment, we take equity in the company and a percentage of sales."

Direct-to-consumer merchandising endeavors can also start on a smaller scale, gradually growing and building over time. With the advent of the Internet and e-commerce, a multitude of opportunities has opened up. No longer are expensive catalogs with high distribution costs a factor for creatives who want to start a mail order business. The Internet has allowed small businesses to penetrate a worldwide market quite cost-effectively. Because the Web also operates on real time, new product lines can be displayed instantaneously, offering a fresh view for buyers who frequent the site. Print-on-demand has also lowered the cost of warehousing and production, making the financial investment more affordable than before. "The technology is enabling us to do things we would never have imagined a year or two ago," shares Riordon. "It is pretty exciting." Some of the products being produced are T-shirts, posters and limited-edition prints, mugs, plates, collectibles, greeting cards, paper products, and games.

Other viable areas to target are the ever-growing leisure markets. "In the United Kingdom over the past decade, people's lifestyles have changed. Leisure time, which suffered in the nineties workplace, is now becoming a more important part of our lives," acknowledges Mark Bottomley of Origin. "It's a huge market,

which means new products that will require innovative promotion." Lars Harmsen of Starshot adds, "A lot of people have shorter workweeks and more free time to consume. They are much more in touch with nutrition, travel, and entertainment. We started a company three years ago named Starshot. The main focus is dealing with sports and leisure."

To penetrate the marketplace, Starshot designed and produced *Byke Style Mag*, a cutting-edge magazine aimed at the bicycle industry. "The magazine has given us a lot of contacts in the business," Harmsen admits. "Clients see our graphic design in the magazine and hire us to do other work, like brochures." Starshot has full control over the editorial content and design, allowing the creative firm to show off their best work throughout the industry. In every issue, all of the custom typography is created in-house and sold under a font house called Volcano Type, another division of the entrepreneurial design firm. The ads that appear throughout the publication are also designed by Starshot—creating yet another additional source of income.

Not everyone has the insight, courage, or stamina to start a new business, so many are seeking other outlets to survive. With advancements in technology, electronic media has spurred an alternative market in which visual communicators can move and grow. Projects include animated commercials, sophisticated 3-D presentation graphics, and electronic collateral such as interactive newsletters and online annual reports, to name just a few. "For a long time, the Web has been dominated by programmers and engineers who know very little about branding, type, image, and hierarchy of message," claims Riordon. "Corporations are at a point where they want the same level of sophistication online that they see in print. We see it as a tremendous opportunity. Like most design firms, we are looking at other ways to promote our services to that medium."

Technology has also created a new venue for the licensing of stock online. Because of the negative effect that corporate stock houses have had on illustrators and photographers, they have taken matters into their own hands and developed some of the best sources of innovative stock available. Unlike the cumbersome corporate stock catalogs that feature generic prefab imagery, interactive, artist-controlled group sites allow access to a vast selection of high-quality work with customized keyword searching and an instant retrieval system, where buyers can purchase from anywhere in the world at any time. If creatives maintain control of their intellectual property by refusing to sign all rights contracts, they can further reap financial benefits from

their work down the road through licensing. When interactive TV, video-on-demand, and shopping-on-demand become mainstream and publishers find a way to make money through online subscriptions, an even greater scope of work will open up.

Every successful business has one eye on the wheel and the other on the future. It is important to the longevity of your business to make time, on a regular basis, to focus on ways in which to keep your company on track and moving forward. Do not get so caught up in the day-to-day routine that you allow opportunities to pass you by. The future will bring many challenges to hurdle, but for those who are willing to learn new skills, opportunities abound. Whether through merchandising, client partnerships, or the multitude of options available in the new media arena, creatives will continue to flourish, and they will do so on their own terms.

With the advancements in technology, electronic media has spurred an alternative market for visual communicators to move and grow.

merchandising endeavor

For years, the team at Form had been designing merchandise for musical bands in the United Kingdom and struggling to persuade them to do anything creative. "We decided to create our own designs and be our own client, setting up a separate company called Uniform," remarks creative director Paula Benson. "It supports itself and allows us to express ourselves without client restraints. It is also great to work with another medium apart from paper or screen."

About fifteen designs were created and sampled onto T-shirts, with the best going into full production. Safe-T UniForm, a custom-designed line of T-shirts, is all about safety. "We love utilitarian signage such as airport graphics, hazard symbols, and safety signs," offers Benson. The unusual print placements, interesting use of materials, and strong graphic appeal make the line of streetwear a must-have.

To promote and launch the Safe-T line, UniForm sent promotional T-shirts to bands, disc jockeys, celebrities, and the press. "This gave us something to write about on our Web site," adds Benson. "It also gave a celebrity endorsement to the range." To be eye-catching, the highly graphic T-shirts were delivered in clear air packs along with a poster, presenting the eccentric line in a far from traditional way. As a play on the overall safety theme, the back of the poster demonstrated how the shirts could be used in case of emergency—as a sling,

bandage, breathing aid, smoke excluder, or fire blanket. With the tagline "Be seen, be safe," the unique line of streetwear gives new meaning to wearing a shirt. The humorous disclaimer "UniForm accepts no responsibility for any misguided or delusional people who may injure or cause harm to themselves by attempting to use their garment in such a way as shown above" just adds to the overall appeal of Safe-T. The innovative promotion attracted a lot of attention, building massive Web site traffic and landing numerous feature stories for the newly formed company.

UniForm, which started as a sideline, has now become a booming business with global distribution, selling through their fully secure Web site (www.uniform.uk.com) and a number of retailers in the United Kingdom. "A lot of Form's clients have seen what we are doing with UniForm and have asked us to design clothing lines for them," acknowledges Benson. "Since we now have a lot of experience in what works and what doesn't, our clients can buy into our experience when they commission us." Because of the success of UniForm, Form is now exploring other merchandising avenues.

FIRM: UNIFORM/FORM

CREATIVE DIRECTORS:
    PAULA BENSON AND PAUL WEST

DESIGNER: CLAIRE WARNER

PRINTING: HERONSWOOD

MANUFACTURER:
    GREEN ISLAND (AIR PACK)

entrepreneurial mindset

With a passion for fashion, partners Pam Williams and Lisa House decided to diversify their business and open a high-end retail boutique selling signature apparel and accessories. Before they took on the venture, they thought hard about what they really wanted to create—and, most important, did their homework. "We started by doing qualitative research on the name of the store," says creative director Pam Williams. "We were interested in understanding how Moo would play among potential shoppers." The next step was to determine the customer profile—a confident woman with a keen sense of humor. "She is someone who knows what she likes and seeks out pieces that are unique and fresh," adds Williams. "Our customer needed to respond to the name in a positive way. If she laughed, she got what the store was about. Fashion is fun, and our name needed to reflect that."

To launch their new retail endeavor, Williams and House needed a flexible core identity system that not only conveyed the true spirit of Moo but also could be built on over time. "The biggest challenge was visually and aesthetically balancing a sense of humor with important elements of sophistication and style in one identity," Williams admits. To begin the design effort, the creative team researched an array of specialty processes and materials that could add character and distinction to the Moo brand. "The research helped us determine what would be possible and what effects we could achieve," notes Williams. "To us, using just the right materials represents the difference between a bound-button hole and a machine-stitched version."

When it came to color, the team looked toward classic simplicity. "A great wardrobe starts with basic black and white pieces, and so too would this identity," Williams interjects. "Accent colors were later incorporated, much like the way accessories add a finishing touch to an ensemble." To bring in the look of fabric, highly textured materials and knits were purchased, scanned into the computer, and added as accents to the various collateral. The resulting identity includes custom die-cut stationery, hang tags, and grommet-bound gift certificates; each element utilizes embossing, foil stamping, and perforation of Via Pure Smooth white paper. The business system is not only fun but sophisticated, a true reflection of the Moo brand.

To ride the wave of instability in the marketplace, many are diversifying into other areas and, essentially, becoming their own client.

FIRM: WILLIAMS AND HOUSE

CREATIVE DIRECTOR: PAM WILLIAMS

DESIGNER: RICH HOLLANT, CO:LAB

PRINTING: THE POND-EKBERG COMPANY

SPECIAL TECHNIQUES: THE POND-EKBERG COMPANY

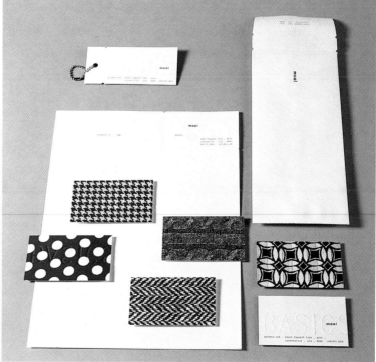

in our leisure

Starshot, a company that specializes in the sports and leisure market, was formed when a retired biking professional, Kai Stuht, joined forces with MAGMA, a cutting-edge German design firm. "In the beginning, the idea of Starshot was that Kai Stuht would go out and take photographs of biking—specifically mountain and racing—stars," explains creative director Lars Harmsen. "The pictures, along with one editorial interview, were put together in a small magazinelike booklet and sent to various trade publications in the biking industry in Europe and the United States." Each booklet came complete with a CD-ROM containing both the text and images so interested publications could easily integrate the content into their magazine. "We saw that selling to magazines was a hard business, and we had to be on the phone a lot," adds Harmsen. "So we decided to create our own magazine, and that is how we came up with *Byke Style Mag*."

With complete creative freedom, the design team at Starshot push themselves each issue to produce something innovative, boasting the latest techniques. *Byke Style Mag* 4, for instance, opens with an orange fluorescent ink accent by a holographic foil-stamped logo that is also embossed off the surface in select areas. To make the cover photo pop, the same holographic material is applied to the surface as a gold foil stamp. Inside, the excitement continues as foil stamps are creatively mixed with fluorescent, metallic, and process offset colors. To achieve different tones of silver, various inks are printed with the metallic color later applied on top.

Byke Style Mag 5, also an experiment in production, uses glitter to accent key graphics and action imagery. To achieve the effect, glitter is added to a gloss varnish in varying degrees. The varnish and glitter mixture is then applied through a silk-screen printing process to various areas throughout the magazine. According to Harmsen, the glitter works best on a darker solid or an area of continuous tone. Because the magazine uses an array of techniques and equipment, the layout must be carefully planned to make everything come together smoothly in the end. In many cases, each thirty-two page signature must go through numerous processes: offset printing, silk-screen printing, and foil stamping. "I need to know exactly which colors and techniques will be printed on each page. It is a lot of work because of the different printing machines being used," comments Harmsen.

The magazines are distributed free to the public through large bike retailers, mail order companies, and railway stations all over Germany. "We made a joint venture with a bicycle builder who has a big distribution net," notes Harmsen. A total of twenty-five thousand magazines are distributed four times a year. "They are a great way for us to explore and show our work," Harmsen concludes. "We have gotten projects from well-known companies in the industry who have seen our magazine." They were recently asked to design a signature line of aluminum water bottles for SIGG Switzerland's 2003 collection. By creating a vehicle for their work to penetrate the marketplace, Starshot built name and market recognition in the industry, attracting top clients to their doorstep.

It is important to the longevity of your business to make time, on a regular basis, to focus on ways in which to keep your company on track and moving forward.

FIRM: STARSHOT

CREATIVE DIRECTOR: LARS HARMSEN

DESIGNER: TINA WEISSER

TYPE DESIGNERS: LARS HARMSEN, BORIS KAHL, AND FLORIAN GÄRTNER (WWW.VOLCANO-TYPE.DE)

PHOTOGRAPHY: KAI STUHT

EDITORIAL: KAI STUHT (EDITOR IN CHIEF), TOM LINTHALER, FRIEDER MEIER, CHRIS STEURER, AND TINA WEISSER

PRINTING AND BINDERY: ENGELHARDT & BAUER (STARSHOT *BYKE STYLE MAG 4*) AND GREISER DRUCK GMBH & CO. KG (STARSHOT *BYKE STYLE MAG 5*)

SPECIAL TECHNIQUES: ARBEITSKREIS PRÄGEFOLIENDRUCK (HOLOGRAPHIC HOT FOIL STAMP AND EMBOSSING), RIEKER DRUCKVEREDELUNG GMBH & CO. KG (SILK-SCREENING OF GLITTER INK), AND FRANZ SCHMITT KG (HOT FOIL STAMP)

MANUFACTURER: SIGG SWITZERLAND AG (WATER BOTTLES)

directory

OF SUPPLIERS AND MANUFACTURERS

a

Acco New Zealand Ltd.
P.O. Box 13342
Wellington
New Zealand
TEL 0064 4 232 7123
FAX 0064 4 232 7157

Action Envelope
245 Adams Boulevard
Farmingdale, NY 11735
USA
TEL (800) 653-1705
FAX (631) 249-5484

AKD
Savska 31
10 000 Zagreb
Croatia

Alderson Brothers Printers Ltd.
Columbian House
Unit 2 Pool Road
West Molesey, Surrey KT8 2NZ
England, UK

**American Printing
& Envelope Company**
900 Broadway
New York, NY 10003
USA
TEL (800) 221-9403

Ames Letterpress
13026 Saticoy Street
North Hollywood, CA 91605
USA
TEL (818) 982-9008
FAX (818) 982-9698

Amex Die-Cutting
2454 North Chico Avenue
South El Monte, CA 91733
USA
TEL (626) 579-6800
FAX (626) 350-6111

Anaglyphic Imaging
c/o Gerald &
Cullen Rapp, Inc.
108 East 35th Street
New York, NY 10016
USA
TEL (212) 889-3337
FAX (212) 889-3341
www.rappart.com
gerald@rappart.com

Anderson Lithograph
3217 South Garfield Avenue
Los Angeles, CA 90040
USA
TEL (323) 727-7767
FAX (323) 722-2328

Anstey Bookbinding, Inc.
50 Hollinger Road
Toronto, ON M4B 3G5
Canada
TEL (416) 757-9991
FAX (416) 757-2040

APS Group
Chetham House
Bird Hall Lane
Cheadle Heath
Cheshire SK3 0ZP
England, UK

Arbeitskreis Prägefoliendruck
Nepperberg 3
D-73525 Schwäbisch-Gmünd
Germany
TEL +49-7171-4183
FAX +49-7171-949337

Arc Colourprint Ltd.
16/3 Timber Bush
Edinburgh EH6 6QH
Scotland, UK
TEL. +44(0) 131 555 5459
FAX. +44(0)131 554 3309

A. R. Printers Ltd.
8 Rival Street
Tel Aviv, Israel
TEL 972-3-6879272

Artcraft, Inc.
P.O. Box 35063
Des Moines, IA 50315-0301
USA
TEL (515) 285-3550

Associated Bags Co.
400 West Boden Street
Milwaukee, WI
USA
TEL (800) 926-6100

Atlas Press, Inc.
412 High Plain Street, Unit #18
Walpole, MA 02081
USA
TEL (508) 668-3383
FAX (508) 668-3838
www.atlaspressinc.com

Aubrey Imaging
(anaglyph imaging consultant)
c/o Gerald & Cullen Rapp, Inc.
108 East 35th Street
New York, NY 10016
USA
TEL (212) 889-3337
FAX (212) 889-3341
www.rappart.com
gerald@rappart.com

b

The Beanstock Group
707 Gordon Baker Road
Toronto, ON M2H 2S6
Canada
TEL (416) 391 9191
FAX (416) 494 3028

Berica Marketing
50 Grove Road
Blenheim, New Zealand
TEL 00 64 3 577 5569

Big3D.com Worldwide
3D Lenticular Graphics
1419 M Street
Fresno, CA 93721
USA
TEL (559) 233-3380
www.Big3D.com
Tom@Big3d.com

Blenheim Printing Co.
12 Boyce Street
Blenheim
New Zealand
TEL 0064 3 578 1322
FAX 00 64 3 578 2232
info@blenheimprint.com

Blue Dolphin Screenprint
100 Main Street, 4th Floor
Somersworth, NH 03878
USA
TEL (603) 692-2500

Bob's Rubber Stamp
15 Autumn Pond Park
Greenland, NH 03840
USA
TEL (603) 431-2522
FAX (603) 431-5708
www.BobsRubberStamps.com

BOS Print
16 Auckland Street
Blenheim
New Zealand
TEL +64 3 578 7672,
FAX +64 3 578 2077
bosprint@xtra.co.nz

Brymark Promotions
2405A, St-Laurent Boulevard
Ottawa, ON K1G 5B4
Canada
TEL (613) 737-4556

Buchbinder Meister Ludwig Weiss
D 76327 Pfinztal
Germany

**Buchbinderei Mende
Herr Siegle**
Klingenstrasse 123
Germany
TEL 0711-464285
FAX 0711-4800092

c

California Stamp Company
1492 Fifth Avenue
San Diego, CA 92101
USA
TEL (619) 232-5037

Calumet Container
16920 State Street
South Holland, IL 60473
USA
TEL (708) 333-6521
FAX (888) 333-8540
www.calumetcarton.com

The Campbell Group
Pareto Print
60 Wellesley Street W
Toronto, ON M5S 3L2
Canada
TEL (800) 774-9874
www.paretoprint.com
info@paretocorporation.com

Capital Box
1475 Startop Road
Ottawa, ON K1B 3W5
Canada
TEL (613) 746-8171

Cas-Pak Products Ltd.
P.O. Box 22 884
Otahuhu, Auckland, New Zealand
TEL +64 9 526 0086
Fax +64 9 526 0087
www.caspak.com

Challenge Printing
7500 Golden Triangle Drive
Eden Prairie, MN 55343
USA
TEL (952) 903-4400
FAX (952) 942-0973

City Litho Ltd.
Unit 39, Bangor Road
Edinburgh EH6 5JX
Scotland, UK
TEL +44(0) 131 555 1483
FAX +44(0) 131 553 7659

Coast Litho
1845 Pontius Avenue
West Los Angeles, CA 90025
USA
TEL (310) 477-0280
FAX (310) 312-9457

Coburn Corporation
1650 Corporate Road
West Lakewood, NJ 08701
USA
TEL (732) 367-5511
FAX (732) 367-2908
www.coburn.com
coburncorp@aol.com

Co:Lab
56 Arbor Street
Hartford, CT 06106
USA
TEL (860) 233-6382

Colorcraft of Virginia, Inc.
22645 Sally Ride Drive,
Suite 100
Sterling, VA 20164
USA

ColorGraphics
1421 South Dean Street
Seattle, WA 98144
USA
TEL (206) 329-0550

Contact Creative Services
1180 Wilton Grove Road, RR7
London, ON
N6N 1C8
Canada
TEL (800) 361-1672

Corporate Express
Charles and Seymour Streets
Blenheim
New Zealand
TEL 0064 3 578 3369

Creative Beginnings
475 Morro Bay Boulevard
Morro Bay, CA 93442
USA
TEL (800) 367-1739

Creative Finishing, Inc.
1 Concord Square #5
Boston, MA 02118
USA
TEL (617) 721-6303
FAX (617) 247-7872

Crooked Cove
2 Spinney Cove
Kittery, ME 03904
USA
TEL (207) 439-4399
FAX (207) 439-4399
www.crookedcove.com

C & S Sales
13200 Estrella Avenue
Gardena, CA 90248
USA
TEL (310) 538-1219
FAX (310) 538-2814

Custom Display
411 West 157th Street
Gardena, CA 90248
USA
TEL (310) 768-8016

CYRK
1400 Providence Highway
Norwood, MA 02062
USA
TEL (781) 769-2900

d

Decato Sound
26 Elm Street
Dover, NH 03820
USA
TEL/FAX (603) 750-7055
www.decatosound.com

Def. Graphic Productions
Van Diemenstraat 302, 1013 CR
Amsterdam
Netherlands
TEL +31 20-4284777
FAX +31 20-4284778

Die Tech Associates
29 Teed Drive
Randolph, MA 02368
USA
TEL (781) 963-0160

Digit Imaging
284 East Lafayette Frontage Road
St. Paul, MN 55107
USA
TEL (651) 287-5943
FAX (651) 287-7368

Dimensional Design Ltd.
P.O. Box 13-756
Christchurch
South Island, New Zealand
TEL/FAX +64 3 365-2599
www.phillipfickling.com
nemo@xtra.co.nz

Diversified Graphics, Inc.
1700 NE Broadway Street
Minneapolis, MN 55413
USA
TEL (612) 362-2595

Drukkerij Koenders & Van Steijn
Postbus 319, 1170 AH
Badhoevedorp, Netherlands
TEL +31 20-6599259
FAX +31 20-6599670

Dumont Promotional Images, Inc.
2912 Colorado Avenue, Suite 202
Santa Monica, CA 90404
USA
TEL (310) 453-8301
FAX (310) 828-2559

e

Edis s.p.a.
Via Tacito 40, 41100
Modena, Italy
TEL +39 59847711
FAX +39 59847784

Edward de Bono
P.O. Box 17
Sliema SLM01
Malta
TEL +356 21 389336
FAX +356 21 385930
www.edwarddebono.com
info@edwarddebono.com

eLaserworks
558 Broome Street, Suite 2
New York, NY 10013
USA
TEL/FAX (646) 613-0848

The Electric Cave
800 Islington Street
Portsmouth, NH 03801
USA
TEL/FAX (603) 433-0892
www.theelectriccave.com

Elwood Packaging, Inc.
5200 West Roosevelt Road
Chicago, IL 60644
USA
TEL (866) 635-9663

Engelhardt & Bauer
Kaeppelstraße 10
D-76131 Karlsruhe
Germany
TEL +49-721-96 226 0
FAX +49-721-96 226 81
www.printkult.de

f

Faber-Castell
Faber-Castell Strasse 17
95179 Geroldsgrun
Germany
TEL 0911-99650
FAX 0911-9965760

Fisher-Price
636 Girard Avenue
East Aurora, NY 14052
USA

Foremost Graphics
2921 Wilson Drive NW
Grand Rapids, MI 49544
USA
TEL (616) 453-4747

Fox Press, Inc.
c/o of Gerald & Cullen Rapp, Inc.
108 East 35th Street
New York, NY 10016
USA
TEL (212) 889-3337
FAX (212) 889-3341
www.rappart.com
gerald@rappart.com

Franz Schmitt KG
Industriestraße 4
77833 Ottersweier
Germany
TEL 07223 2802119

g

GAC/Allied
832 Fidalgo Street
Seattle, WA 98108
USA
TEL (206) 767-4190
FAX (206) 763-3034

Gavin Martin Associates
KGM House
26–34 Rothschild Street
West Norwood
SE27 0HQ
UK

General Bindery Company
Pleasant Prairie, WI 53158
USA
TEL (262) 947-2019

Generation Printing Ltd.
31 West Third Avenue
Vancouver, BC V5Y 3T8
Canada
TEL (604) 254 4488
FAX (604) 254 0408

Glazed Expressions
8826 Swanson Boulevard
Clive, IA 50325
USA
TEL (515) 224-4700

Graphic Arts Technical Foundation
200 Deer Run Road
Sewickley, PA 15143-2600
USA
TEL (412) 741-6860
or (800) 910-GATF
FAX (412) 741-2311
www.gain.net

Green Island
15 Freeland Road
Ealing
W5 3HR
UK
TEL 0870 789 3377

Greiser Druck GmbH & Co. KG
Karlsruher Straße 22
D-76437 Rastatt
Germany
TEL +49-7222-105 0
FAX +49-7222-105 137

Gypsy Office Supply Company
3409 30th Street
San Diego, CA 92104
USA
TEL (619) 295-1553

h

Hamilton Wood Type
   & Printing Museum
1619 Jefferson Street
Two Rivers, WI 54241
TEL (920) 794-6272
www.woodtype.com

Headlight Innovative Imagery
75 Avenue Breezehill North
Ottawa, ON K1Y 2H6
Canada
TEL (613) 728-1988

Hemlock Printers
7050 Buller Avenue
Burnaby, BC V5J 4S4
Canada
TEL (604) 438-2456
FAX (604) 439-1692

Henk Stallinga
Van Diemenstraat 236
1013 CR Amsterdam
Netherlands
TEL +31 20-4200876
FAX +31 20-4207037

Hepadru
Boxtel
Netherlands

Heronswood
Unit 11, Spa Industrial Estate
Longfield Road
Tunbridge Wells
Kent TN2 3EN
England, UK
TEL 01892 678609

Hi-Tec
34 Hachofer Street
Hulon, Israel
TEL 972-3-5560226

Holographic Finishing
501 Hendricks Causeway
Ridgefield, NJ 07657
USA
TEL (201) 941-4651
FAX (201) 941-4453

Hoveys
999 Islington Street
Portsmouth, NH 03801
USA

i

Impact Images
4919 Windplay Drive, Suite 7
El Dorado Hills, CA 95762
USA
www.clearbags.com

Imprimerie Du Progrès
183 Rue Deveault
Hull, QB J8Z 1S7
Canada
TEL (819) 778-2122

Industrial Laser Cutting
#7-7504 Vantage Place
Delta, BC V4G 1A5
Canada
TEL (604) 946 4152
FAX (604) 946 4153

i

Jam Paper
611 Sixth Avenue at 18th Street
New York, NY 10011
USA
TEL (800) 801-0526

Jenco
401 South J Street
San Bernardino, CA 92410
USA
TEL (909) 381-9453
FAX (909) 383-1106

k

Kate's Paperie
561 Broadway
New York, NY 12127
USA
TEL (212) 941-9816
www.katespaperie.com
info@katespaperie.com

Kikkerland Design, Inc.
423–427 West 127th Street
New York, NY 10027
USA
TEL (212) 678-2250
FAX (212) 678-6296
www.kikkerland.com

Knight Print Ltd.
2A Park Terrace
Blenheim, New Zealand
TEL 0064 3 578 7734
FAX 0064 3 578 8098

l

Lithographics, Inc.
1835 Airlane Drive
Nashville, TN 37210-3838
USA
TEL (615) 889-1200
FAX (615) 883-1483

Lowes
2431 North Main Street
Crossville, TN 38555
USA
TEL (931) 707-5900
FAX (931) 707-5916

Lunar Caustic Press
51 Camden Street
Toronto, ON M5V 1V2
Canada
TEL (416) 703-0096
FAX (416) 703-6308
Attn: Bill Morgan

m

MacPac
Barton Road
Heaton Mersey Industrial Estate
Stockport, Cheshire SK4 3EG
England, UK
TEL +44 (0)161 442 1642
FAX +44 (0)161 442 1643

Maran Printing Service
91 Mystic Street
Arlington, MA 02474
USA
TEL (781) 648-9403

Mason Box Company
521 Mount Hope Street
P.O. Box 129
North Attleboro, MA 02761-0129
USA
TEL (800) 222-2708,
(508) 695-9381
FAX (800) 399-3210,
(508) 695-3210

McArdle Printing Company
800 Commerce Drive
Upper Marlboro, MD 20774
USA

Merrill/Daniels
40 Commercial Street
Everett, MA 02145
USA
TEL (617) 389-7900
FAX (617) 389-2835

n

Natureinhand
Handmade Papers & Products
G 7A/11 DLF City Phase I
Gurgaon 122002
Haryana, India
TEL 91 124 5051250
FAX 91 124 5051593
www.natureinhand.com
www.handmadepapers.biz
jatin@natureinhand.com

NC Slater Corporation
42 West 38th Street
2nd Floor, Suite 202
New York, NY 10018
USA
TEL (212) 768-9434

Neyenesch Printers, Inc.
2750 Kettner Boulevard
San Diego, CA 92101
USA
TEL (619) 297-2281, (800) 299-7250
FAX (619) 299-7250

Newman Graphics
60 High Street
Renwick, Marlborough, New
Zealand
TEL 00 64 3 572 8075
FAX 00 64 3 572 8073
newmangraphics@xtra.co.nz

o

On Demand Imaging
9 Post Road
Portsmouth, NH 03801
USA

One Exception
Dollymans House
Doublegate Lane
Rawreth
Wickford, Essex
England, UK
TEL +44 (0)1268 763182
FAX +44 (0)1268 763587

p

Pacific Fasteners
3934 East First Avenue
Burnaby, BC V5C 5S3
Canada
TEL (604) 294-9411
FAX (604) 294-4730
Paper Access
TEL (800) 727-3701
www.paperaccess.com

Paper Mart
5361 Alexander Street
Los Angeles, CA 90040
USA
TEL 1-800-745-8800
FAX 800-651-0008
www.papermart.com

Peggy Richards Handmade Soap
1232 Bush Street
San Diego, CA 92103
USA
TEL (619) 296-5660

Penmor Lithographers
8 Lexington Street
Lewiston, ME 04241
USA
TEL (207) 784-1341

Peter Engel
173 Holman Road
Oakland, CA 94610
USA
peter@cohousingco.com

The Pond-Ekberg Company
660 Broadway
Chicopee, MA 01020
USA
TEL (413) 594-7511
sales@pond-ekberg.com

Plusworks
Van Diemenstraat 308, 1013 CR
Amsterdam, Netherlands
TEL +31 20-6262416
FAX +31 20-6220991

Precision Colour Printing
Haledane
Halesfield 1
Telford, Shropshire TF7 4QQ
England, UK
TEL +044 (0)1952 585585
FAX +044 (0)1952 680497

Printel d.o.o.
Nova Ves 45
HR-10000 Zagreb
Croatia
TEL/FAX +385 1 4800666
www.printel.hr

ℛ

Ram Printing
P.O. Box 900
Commercial Park
East Hampstead, NH 03826
USA
TEL (603) 382-7045
FAX (603) 382-7629
www.ramprinting.com

Rasco Graphics, Inc.
200 Hudson Street
7th Floor, Suite 2
New York, NY 10013
USA

R. C. Steele
1989 Transit Way
Box 910
Brockport, NY 14420-0910
USA
TEL (800) 872-3773
www.rcsteele.com

Reel 3-D Enterprises
P.O. Box 2368
Culver City, CA 90231
USA

RG Creations
939 Terminal Way
San Carlos, CA 94970
USA
TEL (650) 596-0123

Rieker Druckveredelung
  GmbH & Co. Kg
Max-Lang-Straße 62
D- 70771 Leinfelden
Germany
TEL +49-711-75 20 75 76
FAX +49-711-75 24 48

Riverside Medical Packaging
  Company Ltd.
Newmarket Drive
Derby DE24 8SW
England, UK
TEL +44 (0)1332 755622
FAX +44 (0)1332 757722

Roadrunner Press
2320 West Magnolia Boulevard
Burbank, CA 91506
USA
TEL (818) 843-8722
FAX (818) 843-3157

Robbins Container Corporation
222 Conover Street
Brooklyn, NY 11231
USA
TEL (845) 255-2177

Robert Horsley Printing
108 NW Canal Street
Seattle, WA 98107
USA
TEL (206) 547-7950
FAX (206) 547-7952

Rob-Win Press, Inc.
691 Trump Street
Allentown, PA 18103
USA
TEL (610) 776-1691
FAX (610) 776-1433

Romanow Container
346 University Avenue
Westwood, MA 02090-2309
USA
TEL (781) 320-9000

RP Graphics
425 Superior Boulevard, Unit 1
Mississauga, ON L5T 2W5
Canada
TEL (905) 795-1110
FAX (905) 564-2944

RSS Signs and Graphics
1715 South Railway Street
Regina, SK S4P 0A6
Canada
TEL (306) 569-9755
FAX (306) 347-0021

𝓈

Sabag
3 Timna Street
Hulon, Israel
TEL 972-3-5594850

San Francisco Herb Company
250 14th Street
San Francisco, CA 94103
USA
TEL (800) 227-4530, (415) 861-7174
FAX (415) 861-4440

Seattle Bindery
6540 South Glacier Street,
Suite 120
Seattle, WA 98188
USA
TEL (425) 656-8210
FAX (425) 656-4400

Sérigraphie Albion
140 Rue Adrien-Robert
Hull, QB J8Y 3S2
Canada
TEL (819) 777-2761

Shaker Workshops
P.O. Box 8001
Ashburnham, MA 01430-8001
USA
TEL (800) 840-9121
FAX (978) 827-6554
www.shakerworkshops.com

Ship-It
3600 Eagle Way
Twinsburg, OH 44087
USA
TEL (800) 481-3600

Somerset Graphics Co. Ltd.
370 Brunel Road
Mississauga, ON L4Z 2CZ
Canada
TEL (905) 890-2553
FAX (905) 890-7489

Southern California Graphics
8432 Steller Drive
Culver City, CA 90232
USA
TEL (310) 559-3600
FAX (310) 558-3127

Special Screencraft Printing
647 Powell Street
Vancouver, BC V6A1H2
Canada
TEL (604) 255 3178
FAX (604) 255 6517

Specialties, Inc.
702 Russell Avenue, Suite 308
Gaithersburg, MD 20877
USA
TEL (301) 948-5775
FAX (301) 977-7362

Spema
260 Abbeydale Road
Wembley
Middlesex HA0 1TW
England, UK
TEL +44 (0)208 998 0018
FAX +44 (0)208 998 0019

Spin Offset Ltd.
199 New Road
Rainham
Essex RM13 8SH
England, UK
TEL +044 (0) 1708 557511
FAX + 044 (0) 1708 520726

Steel Rule Dies
68E Centre Street
Nutley, NJ 07110
USA
TEL (973) 661-4563
FAX (973) 661-4111

Studio Ink
837 Godfrey Avenue SW
Grand Rapids, MI 49503
USA
TEL (616) 514-1251
FAX (616) 514-1291

Stylex 3D
3132 Rue Francis Hughes
Laval, QB H7L 5A7
Canada
TEL (450) 967-5923

t

Tallent Planning & Lumber
Pickett Park Road
Highway 154N.
P.O. Box 1044
Jamestown, TN 38556
USA
TEL (931) 879-4877

Top In
16 Hacharoshet Street
Raanana, Israel
TEL 972-9-7409950

u

UK Sewing Services
88 Rocky Lane
Monton
Manchester M30 9LY
England, UK
www.sewing.co.uk
TEL +44(0)161 707 7031
FAX +44 (0)161 789 3898

Uline
TEL (800) 295-5510
FAX 800-295-5571
www.uline.com

US Optical Disc
1 Eagle Drive
Sanford, ME 04073
USA
TEL (800) 743-1124
FAX (207) 324-1124
www.usod.com

**USA Print & Pops
    and Anaglyphic Imaging**
c/o of Gerald & Cullen Rapp, Inc.
108 East 35th Street
New York, NY 10016
USA
TEL (212) 889-3337
FAX (212) 889-3341
www.rappart.com
gerald@rappart.com

u

Volcano Type
c/o Magma
Büro für Gestaltung
Bachstraße 43
D-76185 Karlsruhe
Germany
TEL +49-721-9203501
FAX +49-721-9203502
www.volcano-type.de

w

Ward Digital
2-720 Beatty Street
Vancouver, BC V6B 2M1
Canada
TEL (604) 683-0858
FAX (604) 683-1252

Western Nameplates
Unit 5 7201 72nd Street
Tilbury Industrial Park
Delta, BC V4G 1M5
Canada
TEL (604) 940-0070
FAX (604) 940-0757

Wildseed Farms
425 Wildflower Hills
Fredericksburg, TX 78624
USA
TEL (800) 848-0078

Wrapology Ltd.
Liberty House
222, Regent Street
London W1B 5TR
England, UK
TEL +44(0) 20 7297 2022
FAX +44(0) 20 7297 2100

z

Zinco
Midland House
Lower Forster Street
Walsall WS1 1XB
England, UK
TEL +44 (0)1922 723672
FAX +44 0800 028 6370

directory

a

Atom Design
47 Timber Bush
Edinburgh EH6 6QH
Scotland, UK
TEL +44 0 131 476 8044
FAX +44 0 131 476 8046
www.atomdesign.co.uk
info@atomdesign.co.uk

b

Barbara Lipp Illustration
313 Ringgold Street
Peekskill, NY 10566
USA
TEL/FAX (914) 734-8238
www.barbaralipp.com
bl@el.net

The Bark
2810 Eighth Street
Berkeley, CA 94710
USA
TEL (510) 704-0827
FAX (510) 704-0933
www.thebark.com
bark@thebark.com

BBK Studio, Inc.
648 Monroe Avenue NW, Suite 212
Grand Rapids, MI 49503
USA
TEL (616) 459-4444
FAX (616) 459-4477
www.bbkstudio.com
yang@bbkstudio.com

Bradbury Branding & Design, Inc.
11th Avenue, #300-1640
(head office)
Regina, SK S4P 0H4
Canada
TEL (800) 254-7989
FAX (306) 525-4068

380 Wellington West
(Toronto office)
Toronto, ON M5V 1E3
FAX (416) 369-0515
www.bradburydesign.com
ideas@bradburydesign.com

Brown & Company Design
801 Islington Street, Suite 35
Portsmouth, NH 03801
USA
TEL (603) 436-5239
FAX (603) 436 1363
www.browndesign.com
davidm@browndesign.com

c

Capsule
10 South Fifth Street, Suite 645
Minneapolis, MN 55402 USA
TEL (612) 341-4525
FAX (612) 341-4577
www.capsule.us
akeller@capsule.us

d

Dennis Y. Ichiyama
450 Littleton Street
West Lafayette, IN 47906-3013
USA
TEL (765) 743-0440
diad@purdue.edu

Designation, Inc.
53 Spring Street, 5th Floor
New York, NY 10012
USA
TEL (212) 226-6024
FAX (212) 219-0331
www.quondesign.com
mikequon@aol.com

DSM N.V.
Postbus 6500, 6401 TE
Heerlen, Netherlands
TEL +31 45-5782281

dossiercreative
305-611 Alexander Street
Vancouver, BC V6A 1E1
Canada
TEL (604) 255-2077
FAX (604) 255-2097
www.dossiercreative.com
don@dossiercreative.com

Douglas Joseph Partners
11812 San Vicente Boulevard
Suite 125
Los Angeles, CA 90049
USA
TEL (304) 440 3100
FAX (304) 440-3103
www.djpartners.com
info@djpartners.com

DWL Incorporated
230 Richmond Street East
Level 2
Toronto, ON M5A 1P4
Canada
TEL (416) 364-2045
FAX (416) 364-2422
www.dwl.com
smurenbeeld@dwl.com

g

Gerald & Cullen Rapp, Inc.
108 East 35th Street
New York, NY 10016
USA
TEL (212) 889-3337
FAX (212) 889-3341
www.rappart.com
gerald@rappart.com

Good Gracious! Events
5714 West Pico Boulevard
Los Angeles, CA 90019
USA
TEL (323) 954-2277
FAX (323) 934-8312
ggracious@aol.com

Grafik
1199 N. Fairfax Street, Suite 700
Alexandria, VA 22314
USA
TEL (703) 299-4500
FAX (703) 299-5999
www.grafik.com
info@grafik.com

h

Hambly & Woolley, Inc.
130 Spadina Avenue, Suite 807
Toronto, Ontario M5V 2L4
Canada
TEL (416) 504-2742
FAX (416) 504) 2745
www.hamblywoolley.com
bobh@hamblywoolly.com

Harvard Design School
48 Quincy Street
Cambridge, MA 02138
USA
TEL (617) 495-4731
www.gsd.harvard.edu

Heads, Inc.
594 Broadway #1203S
New York, NY 10012
USA
TEL (212) 941-5970
FAX (212) 941-6087
www.headsinc.com
soso@bway.net

i

i_d buero
Bismarckstrasse 67A
Stuttgart 70197
Germany
TEL +49 711 636 8000
FAX +49 711 636 8008
www.i-dbuero.de
mail@i-dbuero.de

[i]e design
1600 Rosecrans Avenue
Building 6B, Suite 200
Manhattan Beach, CA 90266
USA
TEL (310) 727 –3500
FAX (310) 727-3515
www.iedesign.net
mail@iedesign.net

j

**Jason & Jason Visual
Communications**
11b HaYetzira Street
P.O.B. 2432
Ra'anana Industrial Park 43665
Israel
TEL +972-9-7444282
FAX +972-9-7444272
orily@jasonandjason.com

**Jason and Jason Visual
Communications B.V.**
Breedstraat 27, 3512 TT
Utrecht, Netherlands
Postbus 524
3430 AN Nieuwegein
TEL +31 (0)30-604 00 67
FAX +31 (0)30-604 70 91
mirjam@jasonandjason.com

k

Katherine Dunn
7515 SW 34th Avenue
Portland, OR 97219
USA
TEL (503) 892-3363
katherine@katherine-dunn.com

Kolegramdesign
37 boulevard St-Joseph
Hull, QB J8Y 3V8
Canada
TEL (819) 777-5538
FAX (819) 777-8525
www.kolegram.com
mike@kolegram.com

l

Lava Graphic Designers
Van Diemenstraat 366
1013 CR Amsterdam
Netherlands
TEL +31 020 6222640
FAX +31 020 6390798
www.lava.nl
design@lava.nl

Levy Creative Management
300 East 46th Street Suite 8E
New York, NY 10017
USA
TEL (212) 687 6463
FAX (212) 661 4839
www.levycreative.com
sari@levycreative.com

**Lloyd's Graphic Design
& Communication**
17 Westhaven Place
Blenheim, New Zealand
TEL/FAX 0064 3 578 6955
lloydgraphics@xtra.co.n

m

MAGMA [Büro für Gestaltung]
Bachstraße 43
D-76185 Karlsruhe
Germany
TEL 0721 92919-70
FAX 0721 92919-80
www.magma-ka.de
harmsen@magma-ka.de

Media Consultants
461 Kingsland Avenue
Lyndhurst, NJ 07071-2707
USA
TEL (201) 531-8300
FAX (201) 933-6318
www.popandfoldpapers.com
hlhirsch@earthlink.net

Milton Glaser, Inc.
207 East 32nd Street
New York, NY 10016
USA
TEL (212) 889-3161
FAX (212) 213-4072
www.miltonglaser.com

Miriello Grafico
419 West G Street
San Diego, CA 92101
USA
TEL (619) 234-1124
FAX (619) 234-1960
www.miriellografico.com
pronto@miriellografico.com

Mirko Ilić Corporation
207 East 32nd Street
New York, NY 10016
USA
TEL (212) 481-9737
FAX (212) 481-7088
www.mirkoilic.com
studio@mirkoilic.com

Modern Dog Communications, Inc.
7903 Greenwood Avenue N
Seattle, WA 98103
USA
TEL (206) 789-7667
FAX (206) 789-3171
www.moderndog.com
bubbles@moderndog.com

Motive Design Research LLC
2028 Fifth Avenue, Suite 204
Seattle, WA 98121
USA
TEL (206) 374-8761
FAX (206) 374-8763
www.altmotive.com
info@altmotive.com

n

Nassar Design
11 Park Street
Brookline, MA 02446
USA
TEL (617) 264-2862
FAX (617) 264-2861
n.nassar@verizon.net

o

OrangeSeed Design
800 Washington Avenue N
Suite 461
Minneapolis, MN 55401-1196
USA
TEL (612) 252-9757
FAX (612) 252-9760
www.orangeseed.com
info@orangeseed.com

Origin
Chetham House
Bird Hall Lane
Cheadle Heath
Cheshire SK3 0ZP
England, UK
TEL 0044 161 495 4808
FAX 0044 161 495 4550
www.origincreativedesign.com
enquiries@origincreativedesign.com

p

Pentagram Design Limited
11 Needham Road
London W11 2RP
England, UK
TEL +44 20 7229 3477
FAX +44 20 7727 9932
www.pentagram.co.uk
email@pentagram.co.uk

204 Fifth Avenue
New York, NY 10010
USA
TEL (212) 683-7000
FAX (212) 532-0181
info@pentagram.com
www.pentagram.com

387 Tehama Street
San Francisco, CA 94103
USA
TEL (415) 896-0499
FAX (415) 896-0555
info@sf.pentagram.com
www.pentagram.com

1508 West Fifth Street
Austin, TX 78703
USA
TEL (512) 476-5725
FAX (512) 476-3076
howdy@pentagram.com
www.pentagram.com

Monbijouplatz 5
10178 Berlin
Germany
TEL +49 30 27 87 61-0
FAX +49 30 27 87 61-10
info@pentagram.de

Plainspoke
18 Sheafe Street
Portsmouth, NH 03801
USA
TEL (603) 433-5969
FAX (603) 433-1587
www.plainspoke.com
matt@plainspoke.com

Platform Creative Group, Inc.
80 South Jackson, Suite 308
Seattle, WA 98104
USA
TEL (206) 621-1855
FAX (206) 621-7146
www.platformcreative.com

POP and POP
Novomarofska 27
10 000 Zagreb
Croatia
TEL + 385 1 302-4716
FAX + 385 1 302-6820
danijel.popovic@zg.hinet.hr

q

Question Design
15 Rozbern Drive
Eatontown, NJ 07724
USA
TEL (646) 872-0498
FAX (212) 333-2557
REP (212) 333-2551
www.shannonassociates.com
c_noruzi@hotmail.com

r

Red Canoe
347 Clear Creek Trail
Deer Lodge, TN 37726
USA
TEL (423) 965-2223
FAX (423) 965-1005
www.redcanoe.com
studio@redcanoe.com

Reebok International Ltd.
1895 J. W. Foster Boulevard
Canton, MA 02021
USA
TEL (781) 401-5000
FAX (781) 401-4077
www.reebok.com
eleni.chronopoulos@reebok.com

The Riordon Design Group, Inc.
131 George Street
Oakville, ONT L6J 3B9
Canada
TEL (905) 339-0750
FAX (905) 339-0753
www.riordondesign.com
greer@riordondesign.com

s

Sayles Graphic Design
3701 Beaver Avenue
Des Moines, IA 50310
USA
TEL (515) 279-2922
FAX (515) 279-0212
www.saylesdesign.com
sheree@saylesdesign.com

Sensus Design Factory
Sijecanjska 9
Zagreb HR-10000
Croatia
TEL + 385 1 3049010
FAX + 385 1 3634406
Nedjeljko.spoljar@zg.tel.hr

Signum Niehe Events
Postbus 281, 1400 AG Bussum
Netherlands
TEL +31 35-6926868
FAX +31 35-6920092

SIGG Switzerland AG
Walzmühlestrasse 60
CH-8501 Frauenfeld
Switzerland
TEL +41 (0)52 728 63 30
FAX +41 (0)52 728 63 07
www.sigg.ch
info@sigg.ch

S.L.M. doo
Kuseviceva 7
10000 Zagreb
Croatia
TEL/FAX + 385 1 485-222
Luka.mjeda@zg.tel.hr

Starshot
Malsenstrasse 84
80638 München
Germany
TEL +49 89 159 866 20
FAX +49 89 159 866 88
www.starshot.de
harmsen@starshot.de

u

UniForm/Form
47 Tabernacle Street
London EC2A 4AA
England, UK
TEL 020 7014 1430
www.uniform.uk.com
www.form.uk.com
studio@uniform.uk.com
studio@form.uk.com

Untitled
Nick Veasey
Radar Studio
Coldblow Lane
Thurnham, Maidstone
Kent ME14 3LR
England, UK
TEL +44 (0)1622 737722
FAX +44 (0)1622 738644
Mobile +44 (0)7976 420013
www.untitled.co.uk
info@untitled.co.uk

w

Weidlinger Associates, Inc.
375 Hudson Street
New York, NY 10014-3656
USA
TEL (212) 367-3000
FAX (212) 367-3030
www.wai.com
short@wai.com

Williams and House
296 Country Club Road
Avon, CT 06001
USA
TEL (860) 675-4140
FAX (860) 675-4124
www.williamsandhouse.com
info@williamsandhouse.com

Wordslinger
1527 North Hultman Road
Camano Island, WA 98292
USA
TEL (360) 387-9336
FAX (360) 387-0660
brittany@wordslinger.com

WOW! A Branding Company
101-1300 Richards Street, Suite 101
Vancouver, BC V6B 3G6
Canada
TEL (604) 683-5655
FAX (604) 683-5685
www.wowbranding.com
colleen@wowbranding.com

Wright Photography
Fourways House, 5th Floor
57 Hilton Street
Piccadilly, Manchester M1 2EJ
England, UK
TEL/FAX 0161 236 3646

about the author

Lisa L. Cyr is an illustrator/designer, writer, and national lecturer. Her clients include advertising agencies, corporations, and publishers. She speaks actively at universities, professional organizations, and industry conferences across the United States about successful promotional strategies, marketing opportunities, and entrepreneurial endeavors for designers and illustrators. In addition to her speaking engagements, Cyr writes for many industry trade publications, including *Communication Arts*, *Step Inside Design*, *How*, *3D*, and *Applied Arts*, to name a few. Her articles range from revealing issues that face the industry to featuring top talent in the design and illustration business. Her recent book, *Brochure Design That Works* (Rockport Publishers, 2002), features top national and international promotional work with sidebars and special sections that go beyond the basics to explore the strategic and innovative thinking behind each project. Cyr is a graduate of the Massachusetts College of Art (BFA) and Syracuse University (MA). Her creative work has been exhibited both nationally and internationally and in the permanent collection of the Museum of American Illustration. Cyr is an artist member of the Society of Illustrators, New York City, and the Illustrators Partnership of America. She works in partnership with her husband, Christopher Short, a three-dimensional graphic illustrator and animator.